The Frick Collection, New York

The Frick Collection
1 East 70th Street
New York, NY 10021
USA
Tel.: (+1) 212-288-0700
www.frick.org

The Frick Collection, New York

Colin B. Bailey, *Associate Director and Peter Jay Sharp Chief Curator*,
Susan Grace Galassi, *Senior Curator*, Charlotte Vignon, *Associate Curator for Decorative Arts*,
Margaret Iacono, *Assistant Curator*, Joseph Godla, *Conservator*,
Caitlin F. Henningsen, *Curatorial Assistant*, Joanna Sheers, *Curatorial Assistant*,
Susannah Rutherglen, *Andrew W. Mellon Curatorial Fellow*,
Pablo Pérez d'Ors, *Andrew W. Mellon Curatorial Fellow*

Fondation BNP PARIBAS, Paris
The Frick Collection, New York
Réunion des musées nationaux

Acknowledgments
We owe a debt of gratitude to those who have lent their support to this publication. We
are particularly grateful to Jean-Jacques Goron, Délégué Général Adjoint, Fondation BNP
Paribas, for suggesting and sponsoring this publication; to Peter Ruyffelaere, Editor at Large,
Ludion, for supervising its production; to Michael Bodycomb, Photographer at The Frick
Collection, for his superlative photographs of the rooms and artworks in the Collection;
to Nicholas Wise, Curatorial Assistant at the Frick, for his research on the artworks in the
Collection; and to Tony Waddingham for his elegant design of this volume. In addition to
the authors cited on the title page, we want to thank Denise Allen, Curator, Elaine Koss,
Editor in Chief, Julie Di Filippo, Assistant Editor, and Serena Rattazzi, volunteer, for their
work on the text.

Contents

Foreword

From the beginning, the house that Henry Clay Frick built in 1914 at 1 East 70th Street was intended to serve as a museum—following the deaths of the founder and his wife—"for the use and benefit of all persons whomsoever." But the house was also a home to Frick, his wife, Adelaide, his daughter Helen Clay (less so to his son, Childs), and twenty-seven servants. Once construction of Thomas Hastings's neoclassical Indiana limestone mansion ended and the interiors began to take shape, Frick became more keenly aware of how sculpture, furniture, and the decorative arts might enhance the rooms and halls in which his Old Master paintings as well as his nineteenth-century pictures hung. Gradually, the same insistence on quality that had long marked his activity as a collector of paintings was applied to his selection of objects for the furnishing of the major ground-floor rooms. The taste and discrimination that guided Frick during his lifetime have been maintained by the trustees and family members who transformed his mansion into a museum and have overseen the growth of the Collection, through gifts and purchases, during the past three-quarters of a century.

Our visitors today love the Frick for its unparalleled domestic setting, its peerless collection of masterpieces of European art in all media, and the romance of its association with America's Gilded Age. While a lively roster of loan exhibitions, lectures, seminars, and concerts maintains the institution's commitment to education and research, it is the extraordinarily high quality of the permanent collection and its arrangement within the rooms, halls, and galleries of the Frick that makes the greatest impression on our public. It is therefore a particular pleasure for me to introduce the latest book devoted to The Frick Collection in which the reader will find succinct and up-to-date discussions of the founder and the house he built. Above all, it contains studies of a selection of the masterpieces that he acquired, along with those that entered the collection after his death. The text in this volume has been contributed by our curators, each of whom is a specialist in his or her given area, and reflects the latest scholarship available. We are delighted to participate in the prestigious series established by the Fondation BNP Paribas. It is gratifying to know that this beautifully produced and meticulously edited book will serve as a fitting souvenir of a visit to the Frick and inspire its readers to return often.

Anne L. Poulet

Director, The Frick Collection

1. The Oval Room, looking into the East Gallery

From Mansion to Museum: The Frick Collection at 1 East 70th Street

Mr. Frick's most splendid inheritance from a long line of outdoor-bred ancestors was an exceptionally rugged constitution. His shoulders were broad for his medium height, his chest was very deep and the lines of his torso were hardly less classical than those drawn of Hercules by a student of the master Lycippus.—George Harvey, *Henry Clay Frick, The Man*, 1928

I go to see him and talk until I am nervous. When I stop talking he gazes at me in silence in the most disconcerting way. Then I make a few more remarks, which are always received in silence; and when I come away I am exhausted of all nervous energy.—Thomas Hastings to James Howard Bridge, Frick's secretary, June 1912

The two reminiscences quoted above are from men who knew Henry Clay Frick as well as any outside his family circle—Harvey was his official biographer, Hastings the architect of his mansion at 1 East 70th Street—and they give some sense of the impenetrability of Frick's personality and the difficulties the historian faces when examining him as a collector. In addition to this are certain romantic misconceptions regarding The Frick Collection that have remained current to this day. Contrary to what is often assumed, The Frick Collection is one whose arrangement is not frozen in time. The house itself has been refurbished and added to on three occasions. Between 1931 and 1935 John Russell Pope's extensions converted the mansion into a museum, adding [3] the Oval Room, East Gallery, Garden Court, and Music Room, thereby almost [1, 4, 5]

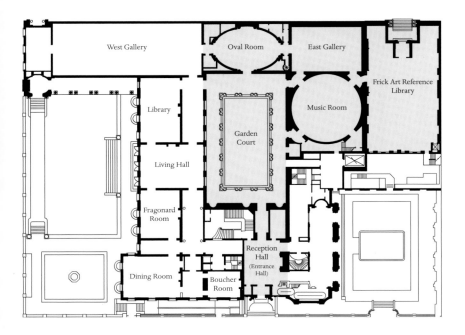

2. Aeolian organ in the Stair Hall, viewed from the South Hall

3. First-floor plan of The Frick Collection, with John Russell Pope's extensions highlighted

4. The East Gallery

5. The Garden Court

6. View of the 70th Street Garden

doubling the size of the building and creating the institution as we know it today. Between 1975 and 1977 a one-story pavilion was added to the southeast wing, whose lower floor, enlivened by Russell Page's 70th Street Garden, has since functioned as the special exhibitions galleries. Currently, Hastings's Loggia and Gallery overlooking Fifth Avenue are being enclosed to create a new Portico Gallery that will house ceramics and sculpture.

No less than the mansion, the Collection itself has grown considerably since Frick's death on December 2, 1919, with many masterpieces acquired by the Board of Trustees in the following decades. Ingres's *Comtesse d'Haussonville* entered the collection in 1927, Constable's *White Horse* in 1943, Memling's *Portrait of a Man* in 1968. The Frick Collection still makes occasional purchases—Watteau's *Portal of Valenciennes* was acquired in 1991, Clodion's *Dance of Time, Three Nymphs Supporting a Clock* in 2006—and its holdings have grown even more actively through gifts and bequests, such as Liotard's *Trompe l'Oeil* (1997), Houdon's *Madame His* (2007), and the timepieces from Winthrop Kellogg Edey's collection (1999).

Nothing could be further from the truth than the idea of "The Frick mausoleum," as Bernard and Mary Berenson spitefully christened the collection in December 1920. Yet it is Frick's selection of superb Old Masters and nineteenth-century paintings, along with the sculpture, furniture, and decorative arts of comparable quality and significance that he acquired in the last years of his life, that has established the character of this house museum and set the standard for the growth of the collection by future generations of trustees, museum directors, and curators.

Henry Clay Frick was born, from relatively modest Mennonite stock, on December 19, 1849, in West Overton, a rural community in southwestern Pennsylvania. The second child of an immigrant farmer who married the daughter of a flour merchant and whisky distiller, Frick worked as a salesman in one of Pittsburgh's most prominent stores and became the well-paid chief bookkeeper for the family distillery; he retained an expertise in accounting for the rest of his life. West Overton was eight miles north of Connellsville, a center in the fledgling iron industry, whose rich coal beds yielded seams of high-grade bituminous coal, ideal for coking. In March 1871 Frick, in partnership with a cousin, invested family money to acquire low-priced coking fields and build fifty coke ovens. Within a decade, H. C. Frick Coke and Company would operate some thousand working ovens and produce almost 80 percent of the coke used by Pittsburgh's burgeoning iron and steel industries.

Even as a young man Frick was interested in pictures. An officer from the newly founded Mellon Bank, sent from Pittsburgh in 1870 to assess the twenty-one-year-old's suitability for a loan of $10,000, noted that Frick lived surrounded by prints and sketches, "some made by himself and all out of place in this half office and half living room in a clapboard shack." Although Frick's request to the bank was rejected, Mellon sent for a second opinion from a more open-minded mining partner, who granted the loan, noting that the applicant "may be a little too enthusiastic about pictures, but not enough to hurt."

Once launched in the coke industry, Frick moved permanently to Pittsburgh, establishing residence in the prosperous Homewood section of the city after his marriage in December 1881 to the twenty-two-year-old Adelaide Howard Childs, daughter of a boot and shoe manufacturer. The Fricks' first home was an eleven-room, two-and-a-half-story house purchased for $25,000 in August 1882. This Italianate residence, called Clayton, was remodeled in 1891 into a twenty-three-room four-story Loire château, a style popularized during the 1870s in New York. It is now home to the Frick Art & Historical Center.

7. Théobald Chartrain, *Portrait of Henry Clay Frick*, 1896, oil on canvas, 46 x 36 (116.8 x 91.4)
Frick Art & Historical Center, Pittsburgh

8. Adelaide Childs Frick and Henry Clay Frick in Boston on their honeymoon, 1882

Frick and Adelaide had four children, only two of whom survived infancy: a son, Childs, born in 1883, and a daughter Helen, born in 1888. Helen never married, founded the Frick Art Reference Library in memory of her father in 1920, and remained its director until 1983, the year before her death at age ninety-six. Childs Frick's children, grandchildren, and great-grandchildren served as presidents of the Collection and members of the Board of Trustees after the museum formally opened to the public in December 1935.

In May 1882 Frick entered into partnership with the Scottish-born steel manufacturer Andrew Carnegie. For the next two decades, as the expansion of the railways created an ever-increasing demand for iron and steel, Frick dedicated himself wholeheartedly to the joint fortunes of the H. C. Frick Coke Company and the Carnegie Brothers Steel Company. He was a lifelong opponent of organized labor, and his refusal to allow union workers at his mines led to the infamous Homestead strike of July 1892, in which ten men were killed and sixty wounded. In a failed assassination attempt, Frick himself was attacked by a twenty-five-year-old Russian anarchist the same month. He cabled both his mother and Carnegie: "Was twice shot, but not dangerously."

Frick grew disenchanted with Carnegie and became honorary chairman of the board in December 1894. Five years later, Carnegie abolished Frick's position as chairman of the H. C. Frick Coke Company, and the two went to court over the value of Frick's interest. In March 1900 a settlement was reached in which Frick received $30 million in securities. In 1901, having moved from Pittsburgh to New York, Frick became one of the directors of J. P. Morgan's newly incorporated United States Steel Corporation; his official biographer noted that he was the largest individual railway stockholder in the world.

Frick had started to collect paintings seriously in his late forties, advised by the art dealer Roland Knoedler. Between 1895 and 1900 he acquired more than ninety pictures, nearly all of which were contemporary works, by fashionable (and expensive) Salon artists such as Adolphe-William Bouguereau, Jules-Adolphe Breton, and Jean-Léon Gérôme, whose studios Frick and Knoedler visited during their summer trips to Paris. To a banker friend Frick confided that buying pictures gave him "more real pleasure than anything I have ever engaged in, outside business." As he came to spend more time in New York, however, Frick's priorities as a collector changed. He now turned to the Old Masters, and his earliest purchases in this field included modest pictures by George Romney and Jean-Marc Nattier. Gradually, but decisively, Frick concentrated his attention on seventeenth-century Dutch and Flemish schools and on British portraiture and landscape of the eighteenth and early nineteenth centuries. In 1901 he acquired *Girl Interrupted at Her Music*, the first of the three Vermeers he would own, for $26,000. When the Berensons visited in January 1904, Frick was informed that they desired "more particularly to see your pictures than anything else."

Although Frick always insisted on simplicity and restraint in his domestic environment, it was into one of New York's most ornate dwellings that he and his family moved in the autumn of 1905. He rented William H. Vanderbilt's neo-Grec brownstone at 640 Fifth Avenue, between 51st and 52nd streets, for ten years at an annual rent of $100,000. Edith Wharton had called this house the "Thermopylae of bad taste." Paradoxically, Frick would reside longer at 640 Fifth Avenue than at the house he built at 1 East 70th Street—nearly ten years rather than five—and it was while he was a tenant of the Vanderbilt mansion that he acquired many of his greatest paintings.

In the decade that Frick was actively establishing his collection of Old Masters, he was also quietly laying the groundwork for their future disposition.

9. Loggia and end of Gallery Wing

10. Fifth Avenue façade of The Frick Collection

In December 1906, just over a year after settling in New York, he acquired the Lenox Library building and site on Fifth Avenue between 70th and 71st streets (200 feet along the Avenue and 125 feet into the block) for $2,250,000. Four months later he added an additional parcel of land running some 50 feet east through the block at a cost of $600,000. On December 18, 1906, *The New York Times* claimed, in error, that it was Frick's intention "to build a home which shall rival, if not outclass, the Carnegie home, situated a mile further up Fifth Avenue" (today home of the Cooper-Hewitt, National Design Museum).

Around 1911–12 Frick turned his attention to choosing the architect who would build his house. He selected Thomas Hastings, of Carrère and Hastings, architects of the New York Public Library. Frick also sought the advice of the art dealer Charles Carstairs, Knoedler's right-hand man and the director of his London gallery. In early February 1912 Carstairs informed Frick that he and Hastings had already had "several meetings," which had resulted in a dozen plans for the new house.

Hastings was an architect who attached great importance to the floor plan of a building. As such, he may have been poorly served by Frick's reticence and a tendency to have others communicate his instructions for him. Most significantly, Frick refrained from informing Hastings that his house would one day function as a museum. Frick's secretary at the time confirmed that Hastings "appears to have no suspicion that [the home] eventually might be more. As you had chosen to limit his understanding of what was required, I did not feel

14

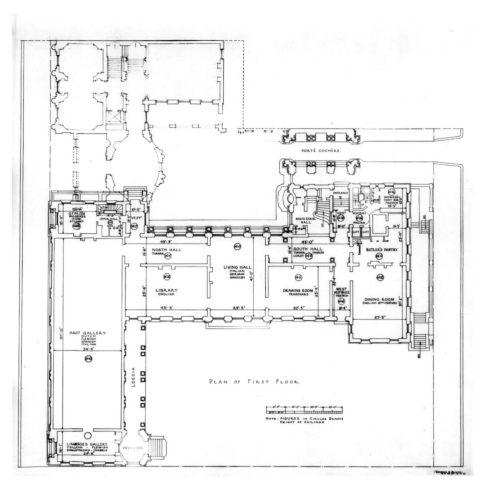

PLAN OF FIRST FLOOR

NOTE: FIGURES IN CIRCLES DENOTE HEIGHT OF CEILINGS

11. Thomas Hastings, ground-floor plan, 1916, redrawn c. 1931

12. Main Entrance at East 70th Street. Photograph published in *Architecture*, November 1914

at liberty to do more than 'suppose' the building was subsequently to be used as a museum."

With Frick's strict requirement for a house "kept simple and conservative in every way," Hastings designed a low-lying neoclassical Indiana limestone building in three blocks, set back seventy-five feet from Fifth Avenue. The front façade on Fifth Avenue was anchored by a central portico, three windows wide, set off by four two-story Ionic pilasters and fronted by low, wide steps and an immense garden. As has recently been observed, this was a surprisingly subversive decision for a new Manhattan residence, since Hastings's design rejected the by now universal custom of building to the edge of the grid and erecting a balustrade close to the property line. To the north, the baroque Gallery Wing evoked Louis XIV's Grand Trianon from the late seventeenth century. The third block of the house contained the Entrance, on East 70th Street, connected to a short wing on the Fifth Avenue garden side. A pair of elaborate wrought-iron gates on East 70th Street led to a porte-cochère and barrel vault, with an interior courtyard beyond.

For the ground floor of the interior, Hastings proposed a dog-leg axial plan, with the three major axes intersecting at ninety-degree angles. Entering through a Vestibule at East 70th Street—no longer the entrance to the museum today—the visitor passed through the Entrance Foyer toward the South Hall, anchored by the Stair Hall at right. Here, a second axis led toward the West Gallery, passing from South Hall to North Hall and uninterrupted by

13. Walter Gay, *The Living Hall*
(The Frick Collection, New York), 1928,
oil on canvas, 18 ⅛ x 22 (46 x 55.9)
Frick Art & Historical Center, Pittsburgh

the central Living Hall. The North and South Halls acted as a sort of corridor
for the principal rooms, which consisted of a Dining Room, a Drawing Room
(later the Fragonard Room), a Living Hall, and a Library, each with views onto
the Fifth Avenue garden. There was neither a music room nor a ballroom at
1 East 70th Street. For music, Frick installed a beloved Aeolian organ in the
Stair Hall; and in place of a ballroom, the picture gallery (the West Gallery)
occupied the grandest space in the house. The second floor comprised the
family's private quarters and guest rooms. Staff and service areas for the
twenty-seven household employees occupied the third floor, the basement,
and the subbasement below, which also housed the family's Bowling Alley and
Billiard Room.

Frick was not at all pleased with Hastings's "Specifications for the Special
Finish of Principal Rooms," which included several ornamented and painted
ceilings. At this point, the English decorator Sir Charles Carrick Allom,
who had recently redesigned the Balcony Room at Buckingham Palace for
George V, made a successful pitch for the decoration of the ground-floor
rooms. He assured Frick that "Nothing should prevent the eye from traveling
always to your works of art, whether picture or otherwise." This was music to
Frick's ears. One cable from him to Allom reads: "Please see that ceilings are
almost plain; Hastings favoring too much carving. Please impress upon him
my earnest desire to avoid anything elaborate."

Frick demanded from his architect and decorator "a comfortable, well-
arranged house, simple, in good taste, not ostentatious." Yet he did not hesitate
to have them use the finest materials available: Botticino and Rosate marbles in
the Entrance Foyer and Vestibule; Touraine marble for the floors of the North
and South Halls; Austrian oak for the floors in the West Gallery. Both Allom
and Hastings understood from the beginning that more than anything else Frick
wanted paneled rooms to set off his paintings. "Do not fail to realize," Hastings
explained in a letter of April 30, 1913, "that we want as much space for the pictures as possible, and that all the paneling has been studied with this in view."

18, 17
13
2, 14

14. The West Gallery

Progress on clearing the site at 1 East 70th Street was rapid, with construction during the summer and autumn of 1913 running ahead of schedule. Frick, almost buoyant, informed Carstairs that "the new home is making splendid progress: the windows are being put in, the plastering well under way, and everything seems to be working out well." The need to furnish his new mansion would also lead Frick to reconsider certain areas of his collection, and in March 1914 he hired Elsie de Wolfe as his second decorator, assigning her the furnishing of the bedrooms and family rooms. As the art dealer Joseph Duveen's Uncle Henry had cautioned his nephew in April 1913: "In offering objects to Mr. Frick for his new home, you should not start out with things of enormous price for him, as he is not accustomed to the idea of Objects of Art of great value." Frick's visit to London and Paris in the spring of 1914 marked a decisive stage in his attitude toward the furnishing of his house. He lunched at Landsdowne House with Victor Cavendish, ninth Duke of Devonshire, and a few days later was invited up to Chatsworth, where, for just over $200,000, he acquired a large suite of what was then thought to be eighteenth-century Gobelins tapestry furniture, intended for the Drawing Room at 1 East 70th Street.

Next stop was Paris, where Frick viewed furniture formerly owned by Lady Wallace, widow of the founder of the Wallace Collection in London, arriving "straight from the golf-course, dressed in plus fours and a plaid cap." He and de Wolfe chose a suite of nineteenth-century salon furniture, pairs of console tables and candelabra, and fine furniture by Carlin and Riesener. In less than a month Frick had spent over $400,000 on furniture, far more than at any previous period of his collecting and at a level commensurate with his purchases of major paintings.

Such was the speed and efficiency of the builders and interior decorators that Frick now summoned Elsie de Wolfe to set sail from Paris to New York a month earlier than expected to supervise the installation of her rooms. "The house," he informed her in June 1914, "will be completed surely by September 1st." Alas, this was not to be. Frick's optimism for a speedy (and seamless) move was shattered by the outbreak of the First World War at the end of July 1914. Very quickly the mass mobilization of working men and the requisitioning of primary materials for arms in Europe had an impact on the final stages of furnishing Frick's New York mansion. It was over the delay in carpets, curtains, wall-hangings, locks, and light fixtures—all being fabricated in Europe—that Frick lost his temper with mounting vehemence. Although the November 1914 issue of the magazine *Architecture* published several photographs of Hastings's new building, with the article reporting that "the most costly and sumptuous residence in the United States has just been turned over to its owner," readers could hardly have surmised that Frick himself was deriving very little pleasure from his new home. Doors were still without locks, he complained to Allom, only now were the backs being put into the fireplaces, and his sitting room was without "a particle of furniture." However, when on November 21, 1914, the Western Union Telegraph installed a stock ticker at 1 East 70th Street, certain essentials, at least, were finally in place.

In the creation of Frick's collection, the legendary dealer Joseph Duveen (1869–1939) emerges at the end of this story as the unquestioned genius in expanding Frick's taste beyond Old Master and nineteenth-century painting. The creation on Fifth Avenue of "Mr. Frick's Palace" had impelled its owner to reconsider the role that sculpture, furniture, and the decorative arts might play in the furnishing of his home and, consequently, in the creation of his future museum. The death of Frick's former business associate J. Pierpont Morgan in March 1913 and the exhibition of 4,100 objects from the Morgan collection at

15. Construction of the Frick residence, aerial view looking west, July 2, 1913

16. View of The Frick Collection from Fifth Avenue. Photograph published in *Architecture*, November 1914

The Metropolitan Museum of Art—a "blockbuster" that opened in February 1914 and would remain on view for more than two years—presented Duveen and Frick with an extraordinary and quite unanticipated opportunity. It was widely known that the collections of the former president of the Metropolitan Museum had not been bequeathed to that museum, and that his estate was not in a position to satisfy the institution in this regard. In February 1915, assisted by Morgan's librarian, Belle da Costa Greene, Duveen brokered the sale from Morgan's son to Henry Clay Frick of sixty-seven of the finest of Morgan's Chinese porcelains for no less than $1,391,000. This was soon followed by *17* the fourteen panels constituting the Fragonard Room, for which Frick paid $1,250,000. The following year, again through Duveen, Frick arranged to purchase choice examples of Morgan's Limoges enamels, Renaissance bronzes, and eighteenth-century French furniture, porcelain, and sculpture for the staggering sum of $5,196,100, to be paid over five years. Despite the rush to complete his house and the disruptions of the previous years, Frick agreed to let Duveen and Allom transform the Drawing Room into a setting for the Fragonard panels. The Fragonard Room was fabricated in Paris by Auguste Decour at the height of the war and was finally installed at 1 East 70th Street in May 1916. "Everything depends upon this," Duveen had cabled to Allom in July 1915; "For we repeat, if room wonderful success our business next year with Maurice [the firm's code name for Frick] will be fabulous."

As the growth of the collection in the last years of Frick's life confirms, Duveen's predictions were exactly right. Between March and November 1916 *81–82* Mrs. Frick's boudoir would be remodeled to receive Boucher's panels of the Arts and Sciences; the ensemble, now attributed to Boucher's workshop, was installed in its own room on the ground floor once the museum opened in 1935. In March 1917 Frick's ground-floor office would be refurbished to display Morgan's Limoges enamels. Duveen also brokered the acquisition of magnificent paintings and sculpture: masterpieces by Frans Hals (*Portrait of a Man*), Vermeer (*Mistress and Maid*), and Gainsborough (*The Mall in St. James's Park*); bronzes by Danese Cattaneo and Jacques Jonghelinck—the last intended for a sculpture gallery that was never realized. The integration of sculpture, furniture, and the decorative arts with Frick's peerless collection of Old Masters and nineteenth-century paintings was one of Duveen's greatest achievements in the shaping of any American collection in the first quarter of the twentieth century. But it was Frick's vision that drove the process; the decision, formalized as early as June 1915, to leave his house and its contents to the public, "for the purpose of encouraging and developing the study of the fine arts, and of advancing the general knowledge of kindred subjects."   C.B.B.

17. The Fragonard Room

On pages 22–23:
18. The Dining Room, with Gainsborough's *Mrs. Peter William Baker* and *The Hon. Frances Duncombe*

Paintings

Portrait and landscape subjects dominate the galleries at the Frick today, a reminder that the collection was never intended to be encyclopedic in its scope; rather, it represents the aesthetic preferences of the founder, Henry Clay Frick, who was counseled by notable experts. Just as telling as what the collection contains is what it does not: scenes of war, nudes, myths, and still lifes are relatively few, since these subjects did not much appeal to the great industrialist, who preferred paintings he found "pleasant to live with."

Frick's assemblage of northern European paintings would eventually boast Rembrandt's *Self-Portrait* of 1658 from the illustrious Ilchester collection and the captivating *Polish Rider* of 1655, three works by Johannes Vermeer, and four by Frans Hals; it would also include pictures by Flemish and German masters. Here again Frick favored portraits—he acquired eight by Sir Anthony Van Dyck and two by Hans Holbein the Younger.

As a consequence of agricultural crises in the 1870s and 1880s, scores of British estate owners were forced to dismantle their art collections; these masterpieces quickly found their way to the homes of American Gilded Age collectors. Frick bought his first British portrait—*Miss Mary Finch-Hatton*, painted in 1788 by George Romney—in 1898; it remains in the Collection today, along with four other works by Romney, seven paintings by Thomas Gainsborough, five by Joseph Mallord William Turner, and other exceptional works by William Hogarth, Sir Joshua Reynolds, John Constable, and Sir Thomas Lawrence.

Paintings by French artists also appealed to Frick. While the atmospheric landscapes of Jean-Baptiste-Camille Corot would retain their allure—four of these purchased by Frick remain in the Collection today and are joined by a fifth acquired after his death—his later interests focused on eighteenth-century paintings by François Boucher and the celebrated panels by Jean-Honoré Fragonard recounting the Progress of Love, painted in the early 1770s. Although Frick tended toward established masters, he was also attracted to the Impressionists and purchased works by Édouard Manet, Hilaire-Germain-Edgar Degas, Pierre-Auguste Renoir, as well as James Abbott McNeill Whistler, an American artist who spent much of his career working in England and France.

Frick's interest in Spanish painting was more pioneering. The eight works by Spanish masters in the Collection—three by El Greco, four by Francisco de Goya y Lucientes, and the incomparable portrait of *King Philip IV of Spain*, *19* of 1644, by Diego Rodríguez de Silva y Velázquez—are among the most powerful works in the museum. In all, Frick purchased eleven Spanish paintings between 1905 and 1914, and the most impressive of these remain in the Collection today.

Frick's first Italian Renaissance painting was Titian's monumental portrait of the often scandalous Italian writer Pietro Aretino. A pair of large-scale allegories by Paolo Veronese—previously part of Emperor Rudolf II's legendary

19. Diego Rodríguez de Silva y Velázquez (1599–1660), *King Philip IV of Spain*, 1644, oil on canvas, 51 ½ x 40 (133.3 x 101.6) 1911.1.123

25

collection—entered the collection in 1912. Ten years after acquiring his first Titian, Frick added another to his collection, *Portrait of a Man in a Red Cap*, dated c. 1516. Also in 1915, Frick purchased Giovanni Bellini's extraordinary *St. Francis in the Desert*, c. 1480, and the elegant *Portrait of Lodovico Capponi*, painted c. 1550–55, by Agnolo Bronzino.

Like her father, Helen Clay Frick (1888–1984) was an avid art collector and, because of her leadership while a trustee of the museum, extraordinary masterpieces entered the Collection: for example, *The Temptation of Christ on the Mountain*, 1308–11, by Duccio di Buoninsegna, and Fra Filippo Lippi's *Annunciation* panels, painted about 1440. Miss Frick's area of specialty was the Italian school, but she also championed the purchase of superlative works by French masters such as Chardin and Ingres.

Henry Clay Frick ensured that The Frick Collection would bear his stamp in perpetuity. None of the works of art he acquired can be deaccessioned or loaned to other institutions. With his characteristic foresight, Frick left a substantial endowment to encourage acquisitions in the early years of the Collection's history. Approximately one-third of the paintings now in the museum were acquired after Frick's death in 1919, and these meet the high standards of quality, condition, and attribution that he set forth and respect the aesthetic and chronological guidelines that he established.

Italian Paintings

The earliest work in The Frick Collection is a small, luminous panel attributed to Cimabue, a founding father of Renaissance art. Acquired in 1950, more than three decades after the death of Henry Clay Frick, the picture reflects the distinctive taste of his daughter Helen. During travels through Europe, Miss Frick cultivated an educated passion for the religious paintings of the "Italian primitives," which her father had largely overlooked in favor of landscapes, portraits, and secular works. By promoting acquisitions from this school, she cemented the Collection's reputation as a rich depository of early Renaissance masterpieces. Indeed, Cimabue's *Flagellation of Christ* is the only picture in the United States by this artist, whom the sixteenth-century biographer Giorgio Vasari described as "born to give first light to the art of painting."

The work represents one of the signal events leading to Christ's crucifixion and death, his humiliation by flogging. Cimabue's Jesus is nearly nude and bound by ropes to a porphyry column. He regards the viewer with his brow furrowed in anguish, revealing mortal vulnerability at the hands of his tormentors. Refulgent with heavenly gold, the scene also evokes the earthly setting of a late medieval square. By transplanting the drama of the Passion into the life of a contemporary town, the artist invites immediate, compassionate participation in the miracle of Christ's suffering and sacrifice for humankind. In 1999–2000 a pendant to the Frick's Cimabue was discovered in a private collection in the United Kingdom. Now in The National Gallery, London, the picture portrays the Virgin and Child enthroned and flanked by a pair of angels. Physical clues such as the wood grain of the two panels, the punched designs on their gold borders, and the patterns of craquelure reveal that these pieces once belonged to the same object: perhaps an altar for private prayer or a dossal illuminating a series of biblical episodes.

The *Temptation of Christ on the Mountain* by Duccio di Buoninsegna, a younger contemporary of Cimabue's, also once formed part of a larger work of art. The *Maestà*, a vast, double-sided altarpiece, was crafted in the early fourteenth century for the high altar of Siena Cathedral. Its front shows the Virgin enthroned in majesty and surrounded by a retinue of saints and

20. Cimabue (Cenni di Pepo)
(c. 1240–c. 1302), *The Flagellation of
Christ*, c. 1280, tempera on poplar
panel, 9 ¾ x 7 ⅞ (24.7 x 20)

1950.1.159

21. Duccio di Buoninsegna (c. 1255–1319),
The Temptation of Christ on the Mountain,
1308–11, tempera on poplar panel,
17 x 18 ⅛ (43.2 x 46)

1927.1.35

22. Paolo and Giovanni Veneziano
(Paolo, active 1321–1358),
The Coronation of the Virgin, 1358,
tempera on poplar panel,
43 ¼ x 27 (110 x 68.5)

1930.1.124

23. Fra Filippo Lippi (c. 1406–1469),
The Annunciation, c. 1440,
tempera on poplar panels:
left panel, 25 ⅛ x 9 ⅞ (63.8 x 25.1);
right panel, 25 ⅛ x 10 (63.8 x 25.4)

1924.1.85

angels, while the reverse once displayed more than forty narrative scenes. The *Temptation*, one of these, recounts the occasion on which Satan offers Jesus "all the kingdoms of the world" in exchange for worshiping him (Matthew 4:8–11). The figures stand on barren outcroppings of rock, while around them appear minutely rendered cityscapes of multicolored brick, stone, and tile. The spectator, too, is tempted by these kingdoms, his eye drawn through their portals, along their winding streets, and into their intricate edifices. Yet Christ himself powerfully rejects the lures of worldly dominion. Shunning the Devil's proposition, he points the frightening creature into exile with an eloquent gesture of his right arm.

In 2006 it was discovered that the two angels at upper right of the *Temptation* were later additions. Originally, Duccio had conceived a tightly focused conflict between Christ and the Devil alone and devoted the remainder of the composition to a spacious landscape with darkening hills in the distance. Perhaps the angels, who according to the Bible ministered to Christ after his temptation, were added at the behest of a religious authority. The work of an assistant, they seem to have been completed in haste.

Cimabue's and Duccio's paintings represent dramatic moments from the life and death of Christ, as recounted in the Gospels. By contrast, *The Coronation* 22 *of the Virgin* by the Venetian artist Paolo Veneziano and his son, Giovanni, narrates an apocryphal tale of the meeting of Jesus and Mary in Paradise. Seated on a sumptuous double throne, the moon beneath her feet, the Mother of God is crowned by her son and serenaded by an angelic orchestra. The setting is one of grandeur and pomp, yet Mary responds with a profoundly modest gesture: head bent and arms crossed on her chest, she echoes her own posture at the Annunciation, when she learned with surprise that she would bear the child Jesus. This glowing image would have had particular resonance for Venetians, who regarded the Virgin as the special protector of their Republic.

Aside from Mary and Christ, the main actors in Paolo's scene are the sixteen diminutive angels surrounding the throne. Their instruments, including frame drum, straight trumpet, psaltery, and lute, are accurately described and correctly played, revealing the artist's acquaintance with contemporary musical practice. There is, however, little evidence of the existence in the fourteenth century of ensemble orchestras in which all these instruments would have been played together. Paolo's musical assembly represents an extraordinary plenitude of sound that, in his age, would have been heard only in Paradise. It offers a fitting accompaniment to the theme of the Coronation, which celebrates the harmony of the universe as manifest in the triumphant reunion of Mary and the Son of God in heaven.

The two *Annunciation* panels of Fra Filippo Lippi, which also concentrate 23 on the life of Mary, were acquired in 1924 as the Frick's first early Italian Renaissance paintings. Lippi, a Carmelite monk who was employed as an artist by the Medici and other prominent Florentine families, probably intended these two graceful scenes to flank a now-lost central panel of a small altarpiece. At left, the angel Gabriel descends on gilded wings into a vaulted church interior, whose gentle gray walls evoke the *pietra serena* stone frequently used in Florentine ecclesiastical architecture of this period. Mary, too, is decked in gold, from the borders of her garment to the edges of her barely perceptible veil; and the approaching dove, symbolic of the Holy Ghost, emits its own gilded halo and rays. The delicate detail of these panels evinces Lippi's skill in painting on a small scale, for which he was lauded by the biographer Vasari: "If Fra Filippo was a rare master in all his pictures," he wrote, "he surpassed himself in the little ones."

Piero della Francesca, another Tuscan artist of the fifteenth century, was well known as a mathematician and theorist, and his paintings embody a rigorous logic of form and color. Piero and his workshop are represented at the Frick by several paintings, acquired over a twenty-five-year period beginning in 1936. The most monumental of these is a deeply contemplative, full-24 length portrait of an aging saint attired in vivid red. It was probably conceived as a lateral element of an altarpiece whose central field is now lost. In this case, we know that the polyptych was commissioned in 1454 for the high altar of an Augustinian church in Piero's hometown of Borgo San Sepolcro and completed about fifteen years later.

Though the identity of the figure in this work has puzzled scholars, he is now usually thought to be John the Evangelist. Standing on a floor of mottled stone, the saint holds and looks at a heavy book, his own Gospel. He is white-haired, and bears an expression of weary inwardness and reserve, accentuated by the lines and shadows of his face. Perhaps his demeanor is meant to show the burdens of his holy labors. Yet the saint's glory is implied, too, in his opulent robe, conceived as a precise volume and modeled in shades of crimson over a complementary green dress. The figure appears before a parapet; this and similar architectural features most likely continued through the background of the entire altarpiece, unifying it as a single gathering of diverse sacred personages.

25 The renowned *St. Francis in the Desert* by Giovanni Bellini—a Venetian whose subtle colorism has been linked to the art of Piero—is rare among the early Italian paintings at the Frick for having been acquired by its founder. Henry Clay Frick purchased the picture in 1915 and gave it pride of place in the Living Hall, where it remains today. Francis, canonized in 1228, was the founder of the religious order that still bears his name. Espousing a life in imitation of Christ, Francis led his followers in dedicated acts of poverty, charity, and devotion. In 1224, while living in temporary retreat from civilization on Mount La Verna, the saint was honored for his empathetic faith with the stigmata, the imprint of the wounds of the Crucifixion.

Bellini's painting is a poetic realization of the spiritual values that informed Francis's life and legacy. The barefoot saint is dressed in the rough brown garment of his order and strides forward with his head raised and hands outstretched, displaying two of the stigmata. He seems to be in transport, bathed in a mystical light that disturbs the branches of the laurel tree at upper left and draws the attention of nearby animals. The low-walled garden behind him houses carefully cultivated medicinal plants, perhaps in allusion to the monastic activities of observant Franciscans in Bellini's Venice. Numerous elements of this meticulously rendered scene have been mined for theological import, and their significance debated. Yet the panel also has been appreciated simply for its "landscape wonderfully composed and detailed," as one sixteenth-century observer described it.

In its position at the center of the Living Hall's south wall, *St. Francis* is flanked by two portraits from the hand of Titian, who succeeded Bellini as official painter to the Republic of Venice. At left hangs the work known 26 to Mr. Frick as the "Red Cap Titian," an infinitely suggestive likeness of a young Venetian dandy. Attired in fur, velvet, and kidskin, he represents the height of stylish refinement in the first two decades of the sixteenth century. Titian flicked his brush to create the white and brown wisps of the figure's lynx cloak and allowed shimmers of light to play over the golden flaps of fabric that meet below his gathered white shirt. Crowning the costume, a soft crimson hat picks up the blushing warmth of the youth's skin.

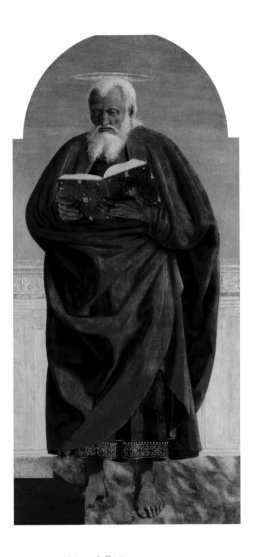

24. Piero della Francesca (1410/20–1492), *St. John the Evangelist*, c. 1454–69, tempera on poplar panel, 52 ¾ x 24 ½ (134 x 62.2)
1936.1.138

25. Giovanni Bellini (c. 1430–1516),
St. Francis in the Desert, c. 1480,
tempera and oil on poplar panel,
49 x 55 ⅞ (124.4 x 141.9)

1915.1.03

26. Titian (1477/90–1576), *Portrait of a Man in a Red Cap*, c. 1516, oil on canvas, 32 ⅜ x 28 (82.3 x 71.1)

1915.1.116

27. Agnolo Bronzino (1503–1572), *Portrait of Lodovico Capponi*, c. 1550–55, oil on poplar panel, 45 ⅞ x 33 ¾ (116.5 x 85.7)

1915.1.19

Texture and color invite the viewer's amorous touch, yet the sitter himself is remote: turning his head and averting his eyes, he fixes his attention on an object unseen or an inner thought. In his portraiture, Titian excelled in the evocation of both individual personality and the defining characteristics of class. The protagonist's clothing, comportment, and ceremonial sword mark the trappings of noble station, yet his physiognomy is undeniably unique. Perhaps he is a poet or daydreamer who, paradoxically, cannot be bothered with worldly things. Eliciting ardor, and then failing to reciprocate it, this unknown figure personifies the elusive aspect of love.

Titian's younger Florentine contemporary Agnolo Bronzino was occupied with numerous commissions for portraits in the circle of Duke Cosimo I de' Medici. Among these is the arresting image of the young Lodovico *27* Capponi (b. 1533), a page at the Medici court. The figure is presented with the meticulous panache characteristic of Bronzino's court paintings. He wears the Capponi family's armorial colors of black and white, their nubbed and pleated textures carefully delineated; his pale, marmoreal skin glows against a scintillating green curtain. Lodovico holds a cameo or medal inscribed with the word *Sorte*, or Fate, partially concealed by one finger in a witty allusion to the obscurity of fate. The young Lodovico's own fate was to be somewhat dramatic: during the same decade when he sat for Bronzino's portrait, he fell in love with a woman intended for another. Duke Cosimo opposed the marriage for three years, but finally was moved by the influence of his wife, Eleonora da Toledo. Upon agreeing to the wedding, the duke demanded that it be celebrated within twenty-four hours.

A canvas by the Venetian artist Paolo Veronese demonstrates a different kind of painterly finesse, that of a gifted colorist working in a sophisticated allegorical vocabulary for a discriminating international clientele. *The Choice between Virtue and Vice* was probably completed circa 1565 for an *28* unknown Venetian patron. Along with a second work of Veronese now in the Collection, *Wisdom and Strength*, it later belonged to Emperor Rudolf II (1552–1612) and then to a series of distinguished European owners before its acquisition by Henry Clay Frick in 1912. These tall, large-scale images probably were not created as an integral pair but rather as portable gallery pictures to be sold individually or together on the art market. They represent full-length personifications of abstract concepts, intended to guide the conduct of their enlightened viewers. Vice, a luxuriously clad woman whose delicate fingertips end in menacing claws, conceals a sphinx and dagger; she pursues a man in white, who flees into the stalwart and protective embrace of Virtue, who is wearing a green dress and laurel wreath. Employing the full range of pigments available in sixteenth-century Venice, Veronese conjures an opulent vision informed by diverse arts. The exquisite rendering of fabrics, for example, reveals the painter's ties to the textile industry: his older brother was an embroiderer or *recamador*. In its marriage of richest textures and surfaces with an erudite symbolic message, Veronese's picture typifies the sensual beauty and intellectual accomplishment of Venetian painting in the High Renaissance.

Northern Paintings

Some of the earliest northern paintings entered the museum's collection following Frick's death in 1919. These important works by eminent Flemish masters are in keeping with the founder's requisite level of quality and also provide a historic context for his later paintings by Flemish, Dutch, and German masters.

28. Paolo Veronese (c. 1528–1588), *The Choice between Virtue and Vice*, c. 1565, oil on canvas, 86 ¼ x 66 ¾ (219 x 169.5)

1912.1.129

Hans Memling was one of the most important Flemish painters of the fifteenth century, who practiced his craft in the cosmopolitan city of Bruges. His *Portrait of a Man*, c. 1470–75, was purchased by the museum in 1968. It is an excellent early example of the type of composition for which Memling would gain renown: a bust-length, three-quarter view set against a distant landscape, here described using aerial perspective. The oak panel has been trimmed on its sides, yet enough of the fictive or trompe-l'oeil frame remains to indicate the sitter's placement in front of it, liberating the unidentified man from the background and placing him in our space. Through the adroit application of translucent oil glazes over denser underpaints, Memling achieved more saturated colors and remarkably realistic forms. Pausing for a moment of reflection, the sitter gazes past the viewer while clutching the strap of his headdress. A tower in the right background may be the church of St. Gilles, located outside the medieval walls of Bruges. Possibly, the round tower alongside the church refers to the Torreman family, whose coat of arms contained similar structures in the family's chapel in St. Gilles. It has been suggested that Jacob Torreman (d. 1488), a churchwarden and the chapel's founder, or another family member, may have commissioned Memling to paint this portrait.

While the Memling portrait entered the museum after the founder's death, *The Deposition*, c. 1495–1500, by Gerard David, was purchased by Frick in 1915, demonstrating the collector's appreciation for the early Flemish masters. Once in the collection of William II of Orange, king of the Netherlands, the painting was an unusual acquisition for Frick, who was not generally interested in overtly religious images. The painting depicts the freeing of Christ's body from the cross by Joseph of Arimathea, who stands at the top of a ladder, while Nicodemus clutches Christ's legs. The grief-stricken Virgin, supported by John the Baptist, tenderly draws her son's limp hand to her lips as Mary Magdalene, identified by her lavish clothing and red purse, holds Christ's body. The habited figure next to the Magdalene may be Saint Scholastica. A final mourner, perhaps Mary Salome, holds the nails of the crucifixion. Human remains scattered across the foreground most likely symbolize the bones of Adam. Their jarring yet eerily beautiful rendering anticipates the still lifes for which future northern artists would be acclaimed. David employs a cool, luminous palette attained through his dexterous control of the oil medium. Thought to be the earliest surviving oil painting on linen, the Frick *Deposition* is a slight deviation from the *tüchlein* technique (tempera on linen), which formed a large part of Bruges's production at this time.

Frick's 1912 purchase of *Sir Thomas More*, painted in 1527 by the German artist Hans Holbein the Younger, was more typical of the collector. More (1477/78–1535), a knighted statesman, social philosopher, acclaimed author, and Catholic saint, was Holbein's first patron during the artist's initial trip to England from 1526 to 1528. The two men may have been introduced by their common acquaintance, the Dutch humanist Desiderius Erasmus (1466–1536). Besides penning the famed treatise *Utopia* (1516), More held a series of political posts under Henry VIII of England (1491–1547), including Privy Councilor, Speaker of the House of Commons, and Lord Chancellor. In disapproval over the Act of Succession, which placed Princess Elizabeth first in line to the throne over her elder half-sister, Princess Mary, More resigned his office. He later refused to support the Act of Supremacy, which declared the king head of the Church of England; consequently he was convicted of high treason and beheaded.

Holbein brilliantly paints a variety of hyperrealistic surfaces and textures— the bristly stubble of More's beard, his glossy mantle with its fur collar, the gleaming chain of office, his supple velvet sleeve—heightening the effect

29. Hans Memling (c. 1430–1494), *Portrait of a Man*, c. 1470–75, oil on oak panel, 13 ⅛ x 9 ⅛ (33.5 x 23.2)
1968.1.169

30. Gerard David (c. 1455–1523),
The Deposition, c. 1495–1500, oil on
canvas, 56 ⅛ x 44 ¼ (142.5 x 112.4)

1915.1.33

31. Hans Holbein the Younger
(1497/98–1543), *Sir Thomas More*, 1527,
oil on panel, 29 ½ x 23 ¾ (74.9 x 60.3)

1912.1.77

32. Anthony Van Dyck (1599–1641),
Frans Snyders, c. 1620, oil on canvas,
56 ⅛ x 41 ½ (142.5 x 105.4)
1909.1.39

33. Anthony Van Dyck (1599–1641),
Margareta Snyders, c. 1620, oil on
canvas, 51 ½ x 39 ⅛ (130.7 x 99.3)
1909.1.42

through a masterful layering of glazes. His skill is evident also in his persuasive depiction of space. Somewhat ironically, Frick installed More's portrait in the Living Hall opposite Holbein's portrait of Thomas Cromwell (c. 1485–1540), the person largely responsible for the former's execution.

32–33   As with More's portrait, the likenesses of Frans and Margareta Snyders were rendered by an intimate friend of the couple, Anthony Van Dyck, around 1620. Frans Snyders was a respected painter of animals, hunts, and still lifes. He collaborated with Van Dyck and other Flemish artists, including Peter Paul Rubens (1577–1640) and Cornelis de Vos (c. 1584–1651), whose sister, Margareta, he married in 1611. Although the portraits were most likely painted before Van Dyck's first trip to Italy in 1621, the sophisticated rendering of depth and the grandeur of the settings, featuring stately columns and billowing draperies that reveal luxuriant grounds in the distance, show the influence of Venetian art, especially the paintings by Titian, examples of which Van Dyck could have seen in Antwerp. The sitters are clad in black, a color befitting Puritan dictates and a customary choice for formal portraits at this time. The artist deftly renders the pair's lustrous, patterned silk garments trimmed with expensive lace, Margareta's fashionable white ruff, her stomacher elaborately embroidered in gold, and her bracelets and rings that underscore the couple's prosperity. Nothing in the portrait of Frans indicates his occupation; his dignified manner and graceful hands imply a patrician elegance. The delicate bouquet of daffodils and poppies in Margareta's portrait may be an elegiac reference: as these flowers were emblematic of death, their presence may indicate that the childless couple was in mourning. The canvases traveled together through various collections—including that of the duc d'Orléans—before being sold to separate English collectors in 1793. Frick reunited the portraits when he purchased them from Knoedler & Company in 1909.

The next year, Frick acquired the celebrated *Polish Rider* by Rembrandt 34
Harmensz. van Rijn. Roger Eliot Fry (1866–1934), a noted artist and critic,
assisted Frick in brokering the sale from Count Zdzisław Tarnowski of Dzików,
Poland. The rider's identity and the image's meaning are still unclear. Whatever
the painting's intended subject, the poised young horseman seated atop his
weathered steed is riveting. The man's watchful gaze and his two swords, bow
and arrows, and the war hammer clenched in his right hand foretell impending
conflict. Using broad strokes of thickly applied earth tones, the artist depicts
a lonely, desiccated landscape with a domed mountaintop edifice at center
and a smoldering, distant campfire at right. The fur-trimmed *kuczma* atop his
head, the elegant *joupane* neatly buttoned from neck to waist, the fitted scarlet
pants and calf-length boots are all consistent with the costume worn by Polish
and Hungarian light cavalry officers. However, Rembrandt often portrayed
his subjects in fanciful mélanges of costumes with little concern for historical
accuracy. Furthermore, little is known of the painting's early provenance, and
the title may be the result of its later presence in Polish collections—including
that of King Stanisłaus II Augustus of Poland in the eighteenth century—
rather than a description of the mounted protagonist.

Frick acquired Rembrandt's *Self-Portrait*, signed and dated 1658, in 1906. 35
This canvas—the largest of Rembrandt's self-portraits—was purchased from
the Earl of Ilchester in Dorset, England, through the dealers Knoedler & Co.
The fifty-two-year-old Rembrandt is posed frontally and gazes directly at the
viewer with eyes that are melancholic and reflective but benign. His outfit
imaginatively combines Oriental elements—the diagonally secured white
shirt, crimson doubled sash, and silver-knobbed cane—with sixteenth-century
historical dress: the square-cut yellow jerkin, embellished neck cloth, and
slashed beret were accouterments particularly associated with artists. Such
garments suggest a regal and prosperous sitter, a wry suggestion considering
that the artist had declared bankruptcy two years earlier. Rembrandt may have
painted the refulgent jerkin to recall the golden clothing reportedly worn by
Lucas van Leyden (c. 1494–1533) and Jan Gossart (c. 1478–1532), thus cleverly
inserting himself into the lineage of illustrious artists from Leiden, his home
town. Rembrandt uses large amounts of pigment applied in discernible brushstrokes to evoke volume and texture. His massive hands—powerful tools of
the Prince of Painters—are vigorously described and seem to celebrate his
manual vocation. While his costume is an imaginative adaptation, his facial
features are recorded in a truthful manner. Archival documents dated 1658
note the ordering (and subsequent breaking) of a large mirror for the artist's
residence, essential equipment for a painter who would compose more than
sixty self-portraits.

Though Rembrandt's works were long admired, paintings by his compa-
triot Johannes Vermeer gained widespread notice only in the late 1850s and
1860s after their reappraisal by the French critic Théophile Thoré-Bürger
(1807–1869), who published under the pseudonym William Bürger. In 1901
Frick purchased *Girl Interrupted at Her Music*, c. 1658–59. *Officer and Laughing* 36
Girl followed in 1911 (and was paid for in part with the return of two portraits
by Rembrandt). The latter, an oil on canvas painted around 1657, records
the intimate encounter between a dashing soldier and a fashionable young
woman. The crimson jacket, black bandolier, and brimmed beaver hat identify
the man as an officer. His silhouetted facial features are barely discernible, but
his posture emits an air of confidence. A gentle and pervasive radiance, stream-
ing through an open window, illuminates the young woman's amiable face,
reflects off her loosely clasped wine glass, glistens against her silken yellow
bodice, and makes the gilded finial on her chair sparkle. The artist evokes the

34. Rembrandt Harmensz. van Rijn
(1606–1669), *The Polish Rider*, c. 1655,
oil on canvas, 46 x 53 ⅛ (116.8 x 134.9)

1910.1.98

35. Rembrandt Harmensz. van Rijn
(1606–1669), *Self-Portrait*, 1658, oil on
canvas, 52 ⅝ x 40 ⅞ (133.7 x 103.8)

1906.1.97

36. Johannes Vermeer (1632–1675),
Officer and Laughing Girl, c. 1657,
oil on canvas, 19 ⅞ x 18 ⅛ (50.5 x 46)

37. Johannes Vermeer (1632–1675),
Mistress and Maid, 1666–67,
oil on canvas, 35 ½ x 31 (90.2 x 78.7)

1919.1.126

various plays of light by manipulating the thickness of his paint: shadows are thinly painted passages, and highlights are formed by thick dabs of pigment. Vermeer suggests spatial recession by placing the officer's dark figure in the left foreground and making him significantly larger than the woman. On the wall above the woman's head hangs a 1621 map of Holland and West Friesland. Perhaps alluding to the soldier's duty to protect his homeland or his territorial aspirations, the map's placement above the woman may also liken her to an object of conquest.

Frick's final Vermeer acquisition—and in fact the last painting he purchased—was *Mistress and Maid*, probably painted about 1666–67. Acting on behalf of Frick, the art dealer Joseph Duveen arranged for the large canvas's purchase from the notable Berlin collector James Simon (1851–1932) in August 1919. The picture presents a young woman seated at a table, her affluence indicated by her elegant coiffure, the fur-trimmed yellow mantle, and the pearls adorning her hair, neck, and ears. The task at which she is engaged further confirms her privileged status as less than half of Dutch women were literate at the time. She lays down her pen on the arrival of her maid, who, dressed in a modest brown bodice and blue apron, emerges from the shadows holding a letter. While the sending and receiving of love letters was a popular theme in Dutch art particularly after the middle of the century, the note's contents and the mistress's response to it are inscrutable. This ambiguity, found often in Vermeer's works, keeps us in suspense, as the figures are enmeshed in a drama whose denouement will never be revealed. The darkened background, with its scarcely legible curtain, seems at first to depart from Vermeer's typical sun-drenched interiors. His masterful treatment of light is revealed, however, in the subtle depiction of a window, not visible in the room itself, but reflected in the glassware on the table. This unseen source of dramatic illumination spotlights the women—especially the softly modeled profile and hand of the mistress—and fixes their gestures.

As with Vermeer's artistic reputation, that of Frans Hals experienced a revival in the 1860s, owing largely to Théophile Thoré's reevaluation of the Dutch artist's oeuvre. Hals's bold handling of paint, dismissed as unfinished and careless by late eighteenth- and early nineteenth-century collectors, was esteemed by Thoré (and later Manet and the Impressionists) for its freshness and vivacity. Frick must have appreciated these qualities, too, since he acquired four paintings by the artist between 1906 and 1917; *Portrait of a Man*, purchased from Duveen, was the latest of these. Although the sitter was identified as Michiel de Ruyter (1607–1676) in the Manchester Art Treasures exhibition of 1857, the painting does not correspond with accepted portraits of the celebrated Dutch admiral. Whoever he is, our subject is shown in three-quarter view dressed in a black cloak and doublet over a white shirt with extravagant double white cuffs. Hals counted Haarlem's wealthy elite among his clientele, and the sitter is probably from this group, as his fashionable attire suggests. The man's long brown hair falls against his white collar, which frames his double-chinned, unsmiling countenance. Hals employs a more detailed treatment—as he did earlier in his career—for the man's face, using concise hatched strokes to model the flesh tones. In contrast, a cacophony of loose, overlapping brushstrokes, applied *alla prima* or "wet on wet," careens across the remainder of the canvas, dissolving into the sheen of the sitter's doublet, the flounces of his shirt, and his clenched left hand, which grasps an ocher glove. This more spontaneous technique suggests that the portrait was painted toward the end of Hals's career, probably around 1660.

38. Frans Hals (1581/85–1666), *Portrait of a Man*, c. 1660, oil on canvas, 44 ½ x 32 ¼ (113 x 81.9)

1917.1.70

39. El Greco (1541–1614), *St. Jerome,*
c. 1590–1600, oil on canvas,
43 ½ x 37 ½ (110.5 x 95.3)

1905.1.67

Spanish Paintings

Though relatively few in number, the Spanish paintings in The Frick Collection leave their special imprint on the museum's character because of their exceptional quality. They also reveal an interesting aspect of Frick's activity as a collector, since, unlike Italian Renaissance or Dutch seventeenth-century paintings, Spanish art was not part of the traditional collector's canon.

Among the first of Frick's Spanish purchases was El Greco's *St. Jerome*, 39 who frowns disapprovingly from above the chimneypiece of the Living Hall. El Greco was born on the island of Crete, and his earliest training took place within the Greek Orthodox tradition of icon painting. He moved to Italy around 1567 and worked in two of the most important artistic centers there, Venice and Rome; in 1577 he traveled to Spain, where he spent the rest of his long career in the city of Toledo. This unusual mixture of learning and working environments contributed to El Greco's development of an eclectic and highly personal idiom. A mature work painted in the last decade of the sixteenth century, *St. Jerome* shows the artist's fondness for rich, sensual color built in layers, in the Venetian manner. At the same time, the proportions and the composition reveal an interest in *disegno* that resonates with the more intellectual approach of Florentine and Roman painters. The saint's features are studiedly elongated, and lines and forms are arranged to enliven a symmetrical axis scheme: the beard, for example, is subtly bent to the right to balance the book on the left. These details convey an impression of intensity and contained movement, as if the viewer's intrusion had broken the deep concentration of the Church Father responsible for translating the Bible into Latin.

As is often the case with El Greco, there are several versions of this painting; this, the finest and the earliest (c. 1590–1600), was in the store room of Valladolid Cathedral when Frick bought it in December 1905. Although El Greco's reputation was not fully established by then, denunciations of the sale in Spanish newspapers contributed to the passing of laws to protect the country's artistic patrimony from avid foreign millionaires. Frick bought the painting under the impression that it was the portrait of a "Cardinal Guiroyal," rather than a religious image, which indicates a market preference for that genre as well as Frick's interest in the subject's individualization and intensity of expression.

Another portrait by El Greco in the Frick, that of *Vincenzo Anastagi*, pos- 40 sesses a similar commanding quality achieved through very different means. This portrait was painted around 1575, near the end of the painter's formative years in Italy. Vincenzo Anastagi (c. 1531–1586) was a soldier and a knight of the military order of Saint John of Jerusalem; he distinguished himself in defending Malta from the Ottoman Turks during the Great Siege of 1565. This is the only known instance by El Greco of a full-length standing portrait, a format that emphasizes Anastagi's imposing physical presence. Special attention has been paid to the velvety texture of the breeches and the reflections on the shiny iron breastplate, a favorite motif of El Greco's. The painter characterizes the sitter by means of a bold shape, pose, and military attire, all of which convey a calm, self-possessed attitude while also suggesting something of the soldier's swagger, whereas the facial expression adds an air of melancholy or stoical resignation. Sometime after El Greco finished the painting, it was modified by a different hand: an inscribed pillar was added to the left of the sitter to identify him, and a cross of Malta was painted on his breastplate to indicate that he was a knight. These details were thought to be distracting, and it was decided to cover them up (reversibly) when the painting was restored in 1959.

40. El Greco (1541–1614), *Vincenzo Anastagi*, c. 1571–76, oil on canvas, 74 x 49 ⅞ (188 x 126.7)
1913.1.68

The gem of the Spanish paintings in the collection is the portrait of *King* 19
Philip IV of Spain by Diego Rodríguez de Silva y Velázquez. When Frick
bought it, in February 1911, the news caused turmoil in the press and the
academic community. Journalists touted the staggering price of the painting—
at $475,000 it was Frick's most expensive acquisition to date—while scholars
had to revise a long-standing assumption: the appearance in the art market of
this portrait, clearly by Velázquez's own hand, showed that a better-known
version in Dulwich Picture Gallery in London was, in fact, a workshop copy.

In 1644, at the height of his career as painter and courtier to Philip IV
of Spain (1605–1665), Velázquez traveled to the border between Aragon and
Catalonia. The king had decided to move the court there in order to supervise
the military campaign against the French, who had come into Catalonia to
support a local secessionist rebellion. The Frick portrait was painted in those
unusual circumstances, which accounts for the wealth of archival information
regarding the making of the image. A narrow room in a war-ravaged village
served as an improvised studio, and the portrait had to be finished in a hurry
so that it could be sent to Madrid, where it would represent the king in a
religious ceremony marking a much-anticipated victory. The result is a typi-
cally understated image that stands out from all others by Velázquez owing to
the military dress worn by the king and the startling freedom with which the
artist summarily conjured up the different textures of the king's costume and
the shimmering silver brocade.

Frick's last Spanish purchase, in 1914, consisted of two paintings by Francisco
de Goya y Lucientes, *The Forge*, and *Doña María Martínez de Puga*. *The Forge* 41
was probably painted around 1815–20; it is a large painting of elusive subject
matter, linked in terms of style to the "Black Paintings" and thematically
to two slightly earlier scenes of daily life now in Budapest's Szépművészeti
Múzeum. It once hung in the famous Galerie Espagnole at the Louvre palace,
the collection of Spanish paintings put together by King Louis-Philippe that
was inaugurated in 1838 and sold at auction in London in 1853.

It has been suggested that the subject of the Frick painting may allude to
a story in Ovid's *Metamorphoses* describing how Apollo appeared in Vulcan's
forge to inform him of the infidelity of his wife, Venus. The toiling smithies in
The Forge would thus represent a satirical (and somewhat misogynistic) warn-
ing to men about the dangerous and fleeting charms of women. Removed
from its original context, the painting remains a powerful image thanks to
its monumental figures and intriguing dark atmosphere, which is almost
monochromatic but for the flash of red-hot metal on the anvil. The handling
of the paint, applied thickly with a palette knife, enhances the rough, physical
character of the scene.

French Paintings

Although Frick had started out collecting fashionable salon painting by contemporary French artists and would go on to acquire superb ensembles of
eighteenth-century French art for his mansion at 1 East 70th Street, the French
school did not appeal to him in the same way that the Dutch and British did.
Many of the greatest eighteenth- and nineteenth-century paintings were
acquired for the Collection by his daughter Helen in the decades following
the founder's death. Interestingly, the small group of Impressionist works that
Frick had purchased in 1914 for relatively modest sums remains among the
most admired in the Collection today.

The Frick Collection acquired its first painting by Jean-Antoine Watteau
as late as 1991. *The Portal of Valenciennes* is among a group of military pictures 42

41. Francisco de Goya y Lucientes
(1746–1828), *The Forge*, c. 1815–20, oil
on canvas, 71 ½ x 49 ¼ (181.6 x 125.1)
1914.1.65

42. Jean-Antoine Watteau (1684–1721),
The Portal of Valenciennes, 1709–10,
oil on canvas, 12 ¾ x 16 (32.4 x 40.6)

Purchased with funds from the bequest of Arthemise
Redpath, 1991. 1991.1.173

that Watteau painted early in his career, and the work's original oval format, still visible to the naked eye, suggests that it may have been part of a decorative series, to be installed in boiserie paneling in a small cabinet or library. Watteau had returned home to Valenciennes—a garrison town during the later years of Louis XIV's ruinous War of the Spanish Succession—in 1709 and 1710 and had filled his sketchbooks with drawings of soldiers at ease between military engagements. In this elegiac and tender painting he shows a sentinel and six other infantrymen relaxing beneath a crumbling archway, evocative of the city's grand fortified gates, which had been erected in the 1680s. The men wear the unbleached uniforms of common soldiers and their casual poses—sleeping, smoking, conversing—convey the camaraderie of a moment of calm between skirmishes. The banality of war—rather than its grandeur or heroism—informs Watteau's composition and is a mark of his originality. The long pike that rests against the royal crest atop the arch at right provides a clue to the first owner (or patron) of this work. The shield may be a punning reference to the art dealer Pierre Sirois, whose shop on the Quai Neuf in Paris was called "Aux Armes de France."

"One uses color, but one paints with feeling," declared Diderot's favorite painter, Jean-Baptiste-Siméon Chardin, who was renowned for his dignified scenes of everyday life and his still-life paintings. Many of the latter were done
43 early in his career, as is the case with *Still Life with Plums*, which dates from

1728, the year Chardin was received into the Royal Academy as a "Painter of animals and fruit." On a stone parapet that appears in many of his still lifes, Chardin has arranged a group of plums atop a flat rush basket, a bottle of wine, a glass half filled with water, and two vegetables, most likely cucumbers. These rustic objects are painted vigorously, roughly almost, against a warmly lit background. The painting's sense of balance and order is precarious; the parapet tilts somewhat, and the single plum may soon begin to roll away. Interested in theories of optics and the psychology of perception, Chardin found painterly equivalences to evoke the volumes of the dark bottle, the reflections in the glass, the looming forms of the vegetables, and the bloom on the ripe plums. Diderot recalled Chardin's telling him that it was not only by sight but by touch that the artist judged the forms of the natural objects that he portrayed in his still lifes, and one can almost imagine him rolling the plums gently between his thumb and forefinger as he set out to paint them.

Born four years after Chardin, François Boucher represents the luxury, brilliance, and plenitude of French painting in the middle decades of the eighteenth century, a period known as the Rococo. In Boucher's *Lady on a Day Bed*, long 44 thought to be a portrait of his young wife, Marie-Jeanne Buseau, he portrays a sharp-faced, dark-eyed woman reclining in a somewhat provocative pose, her stockinged foot shod in a tiny pink mule. The woman is shown in a fashionable brocaded interior, with a chinoiserie screen at far right, a lacquered étagère with Chinese porcelain objects on the wall, and an ornate clock suspended next to it. There is something faintly lascivious in the manner in which Boucher has presented this reclining lady who has been interrupted in her reading and needlework: her right hand is cocked suggestively at her chin, while her left rests languidly between her thighs. Between 1739 and 1746 Boucher undertook a small number of exquisite subject pictures showing pretty young women in domestic situations, in which he explored, in painstaking brushwork, the fashions and luxuries of the day. Boucher soon tired of the care and finish that such works required, however. The pose, accouterments, and doll-like

43. Jean-Baptiste-Siméon Chardin (1699–1779), *Still Life with Plums*, 1728, oil on canvas, 17 ¾ x 19 ¾ (45.1 x 50.2)
1945.1.152

44. François Boucher (1703–1770),
Lady on a Day Bed, 1743, oil on canvas,
22 ½ x 26 ⅞ (57.2 x 68.3)

1937.1.139

45. Jean-Honoré Fragonard
(1732–1806), The Progress of Love:
The Lover Crowned, 1771–72, oil on
canvas, 125 ⅛ x 95 ¾ (317.8 x 243.2)

1915.1.48

features of the reclining figure who meets our gaze in *Lady on a Day Bed* are more appropriate for a finely crafted subject picture, made for the collector's cabinet, than for a portrait, however informal, of a cherished spouse.

Jean-Honoré Fragonard was Boucher's most talented pupil, who maintained his master's brilliant painterly manner during the last decades of the ancien régime. In 1771 Fragonard was commissioned to paint four large canvases for the decoration of the apse-shaped salon—or Salon du Cul de Four—in the

46. Jean-Étienne Liotard (1702–1789), *Trompe l'Oeil*, 1771, oil on silk transferred to canvas, 9 ⅜ x 12 ¾ (23.8 x 32.4)

Bequeathed by Lore Heinemann in memory of her husband, Dr. Rudolph J. Heinemann, 1997. 1997.1.182

new pavilion at Louveciennes that the architect Claude-Nicolas Ledoux was building for the comtesse du Barry, Louis XV's twenty-eight-year-old titular mistress. Fragonard's large compositions took as their subject the Progress of Love, and he devoted almost a year to them, orchestrating a joyful quartet in which the young, innocent lovers play out their idyllic romance in an exuberant and complicit natural setting. The third painting in the series, *The Lover Crowned,* shows the consummation of the couple's love. The garden is at its most abundant, with the orange trees and myrtles—symbols of marriage—in full bloom. The adolescent girl bestows a crown of roses on her suitor, who has already enchained her with a garland of flowers. Their union is memorialized by an equally fresh-faced artist, who is drawing the scene from life on his sheet of blue paper. The garden sculpture that towers above the lovers shows Cupid asleep, his tiny quiver empty; the god of Love has done his work and can now rest easily. Brilliantly conceived and flawlessly executed, Fragonard's series surprisingly failed to please the comtesse. Briefly installed at Louveciennes,

45

the panels were unceremoniously taken down after less than a year, returned to the artist, and replaced by four paintings on the same subject, in a resolutely neoclassical idiom, by the senior and more venerable Academician, Joseph-Marie Vien.

A Swiss artist with an international reputation during his lifetime, prolific as a pastelist and miniaturist as well as a painter, Jean-Étienne Liotard was one of the most probing portraitists of the European Enlightenment, who counted the Hapsburg and Bourbon royal families among his clients. A rarity in his work, the superbly crafted and inventive *Trompe l'Oeil*, bequeathed to 46 the Collection in 1997, was painted on silk attached to a canvas support, which offered the finest surface for Liotard's brushes. The artist was sixty-nine when he undertook this *deceptio visus*—or visual deception—and his powers of invention, no less than his technique, were undiminished by age. Against the background of a simulated pine panel are placed four objects rendered with the most exacting verisimilitude. Two plaster reliefs, hanging from screws to which they are attached by cord, show reclining female nudes attended to by Cupid. The composition on the left is based on an engraving after Boucher's *Venus Sleeping on a Day Bed;* that on the right seems also to have been inspired by Boucher's images of Cupid caressing his mother. Below the reliefs are two drawings affixed to the pine support by red sealing wax. The tiny sheet on the left shows a man wearing a large turban and is inscribed COEFFURE TURQUE (Turkish headwear); next to it is that of a woman wearing a pronged headgear and a ribbon around her neck, inscribed COEFFURE DE ULM, a reference to female costume in this southern German town. Both drawings offer a reminiscence of Liotard's past travels, while the work as a whole is a manifesto of his un-matched powers as a master of illusionism.

Despite his involvement with the French Revolution and his imprisonment during the Terror, Jacques-Louis David won favor with Napoleon, who named him the Empire's First Painter in 1804. Among his most notable commissions from the emperor was *The Coronation of Napoleon in Notre Dame (Le Sacre)*, completed in 1807, but for which the artist received payment only three years later. That he was paid at all was in large part due to the efforts of the em-peror's intendant general, the comte Daru, who had interceded tirelessly on his behalf. It was as a token of his gratitude that in the spring of 1810 David painted the portrait of Daru's twenty-six-year-old wife, Alexandrine-Thérèse 47 Nardot, which the unsuspecting husband found awaiting his return to Paris on March 28, 1810. David portrayed the comtesse sitting in a square-backed mahogany armchair, whose ornamented gilt-bronze sphinxes are just visible. Her opulent green shawl sets off her white satin dress and pink flesh, while also highlighting the delicate emerald necklace and matching earrings. Alexandrine wears a headdress of white orange blossoms—a nuptial symbol—and looks out resolutely, impervious to all distraction. The intensity of her gaze is intended for her husband, who is the only spectator of any consequence.

One of the greatest portraits of the nineteenth century, Ingres's *Comtesse* 48 *d'Haussonville* entered the Collection in January 1927 and was the most signifi-cant acquisition proposed by Frick's daughter Helen to the Board of Trustees. The sitter of Ingres's portrait was the twenty-seven-year-old Louise-Albertine, princesse de Broglie, who had married the diplomat vicomte d'Haussonville in 1836 and was the mother of two children. Ingres had first started work on a portrait of "the lovely, timid little Vicomtesse" in June 1842; the following year he abandoned the composition, then began again, but was prevented from bringing the work to completion by Louise's pregnancy and the family's travels to the Middle East. Between January and June 1845 Ingres worked intensively on the present composition—at least sixteen preparatory drawings survive—

47. Jacques-Louis David (1748–1825),
Comtesse Daru, 1810, oil on canvas,
32 ⅛ x 25 ⅝ (81.6 x 65.1)

1937.1.140

48. Jean-Auguste-Dominique Ingres
(1780–1867), *Comtesse d'Haussonville*,
1845, oil on canvas, 51 ⅞ x 36 ¼
(131.8 x 92.1)

1927.1.81

49. Pierre-Étienne-Théodore
Rousseau (1812–1867), *The Village of
Becquigny*, c. 1857, oil on mahogany
panel, 25 x 39 ⅜ (63.5 x 100)

1902.1.108

and the sitter herself recalled that it took him nine days to paint one of her hands. The artist shows the comtesse in a corner of her boudoir at the family *hôtel particulier* on 35 rue Saint-Dominique in Paris's aristocratic seventh arrondissement. She stands against an upholstered fireplace, two small tufted fauteuils to either side, with a garniture of cobalt Sèvres porcelain and flowers reflected in the mirror behind her. Louise wears a low-necked pleated silk evening gown and jewelry à la Cléopâtre. The cashmere shawl draped over an armchair and the Chinese silk evening bag and opera glasses on the mantelpiece behind suggest that she has just returned from an evening at the theater. Ingres's verism in details of physiognomy, dress, and décor is matched by an intensity of psychological expression in which the viewer is held by Louise's quizzical and not altogether welcoming gaze. As one of the comtesse's intimates remarked, "Monsieur Ingres must be in love with you to have painted you that way."

One of the leaders of the Barbizon school of landscape painting, Pierre-Étienne-Théodore Rousseau was inspired to paint *The Village of Becquigny* after 49 visiting this picturesque region in Picardy in northern France in 1857. He made pen and ink drawings of the village's sandy main street, dotted with puddles and lined with thatched cottages. Over the next seven years, Rousseau worked on the painting itself in his studio in Paris, finally exhibiting it at the Salon of 1864. He may have been inspired by the seventeenth-century Dutch landscape painter Meindert Hobbema, whose scenes of tree-lined avenues and pathways penetrating rustic habitations were particularly admired by the Barbizon generation of landscape painters. While *Village at Becquigny* conveys a sense of calm and serenity—an image of the countryside untroubled by industry or environmental change—the gestation of this work could not have been more agitated. Acquired in 1862, before it was finished, by Frédéric Hartmann, an art-loving textile manufacturer from Munster, *Village at Becquigny* underwent almost continual revisions by its author. Inspired by Japanese prints, Rousseau repainted the sky a bright blue on the night before he submitted the landscape to the Salon of 1864; such was the critical reaction, that he restored this passage to its more muted tones when the painting was returned to him. Although he had paid handsomely for the picture, Hartmann was unable to take possession of his landscape until Rousseau's death. At his request, in March 1868 the artist's close friend Jean-François Millet was charged with "doing what he could ... to give Rousseau's picture the aspect of a finished work."

Manet's *Bullfight* is a striking example of the New Painting that galvanized 50 French art in the 1860s: high keyed, seemingly impromptu, and taking as its subject an episode from modern life. Three bullfighters stand close to the curved fence of the arena—the one in the middle is climbing to safety—as a bull passes in front of them, goaded by the matador with a yellow cape. Manet's bright palette, abbreviated handling, and glimpse of the audience beyond the wall communicate the spontaneity and excitement of the spectacle without recourse to the slightest anecdote. This compact work is a fragment from a large, horizontal painting exhibited at the Salon of 1864 as *Incident in a Bullfight*, which showed a dead toreador lying on the ground, with the bull that had gored him turning to charge the *toreros* in the background. *Incident in a Bullfight* was mercilessly mocked by the critics and caricatured in the press; at the close of the Salon, Manet cut his painting into two pieces of unequal size and reworked both as independent compositions. The larger canvas was transformed into *The Dead Toreador*—today in the National Gallery of Art, Washington, D.C. The Frick's much smaller *Bullfight*, which had formed the upper right-hand section of the original composition, was also extensively reworked by the artist. It is indebted both to Francisco de Goya's etchings and

50. Édouard Manet (1832–1883),
The Bullfight, 1864, oil on canvas,
18 ⅞ x 42 ⅞ (47.9 x 108.9)

1914.1.86

51. Pierre-Auguste Renoir (1841–1919),
Mother and Children (La Promenade),
1875–76, oil on canvas, 67 x 42 ⅝
(170.2 x 108.3)

1914.1.100

52. Hilaire-Germain-Edgar Degas
(1834–1917), *The Rehearsal*, 1878–79,
oil on canvas, 18 ¾ x 24 (47.6 x 61)

1914.1.34

to the actual experience of the bullfight, which Manet may have witnessed for the first time in Madrid in September 1865.

Manet never exhibited with the Impressionists, of which Renoir was a founding member, yet he was revered by the younger generation and during the 1870s was a particular influence on Renoir's large-scale figure paintings. Among the greatest in this format, Renoir's *Mother and Children* was exhibited *51* as "La Promenade" at the Second Impressionist exhibition in April 1876. As its original title suggests, "La Promenade"—The Stroll—is a scene of fashionable Parisian leisure painted in an uncompromisingly modern idiom. Two beautifully dressed young girls are gently shepherded by an elegant young woman along the pathway of a Parisian park; in the background we see various other promenaders, from bourgeois couples to governesses and their charges, even black and white dogs. The three main figures are dressed for winter: the young sisters in identical costumes, trimmed with white fox, the elder girl in a pleated walking dress with bustle and a cobalt blue jacket with fur sleeves. Despite its title, it is unlikely that this is a commissioned portrait, since the three figures were posed for by models whom Renoir may have paid for their services. *Mother and Children* was harshly judged by critics of the Second Impressionist exhibition, dismayed by Renoir's lack of finish and high-toned palette. "From far off one sees a bluish fog, from which six chocolate pastilles forcefully emerge. What can this be? As one gets closer one realizes that the pastilles are the eyes of three people and the fog a mother and her young daughters."

Purchased by Frick in the same year (1914) as the paintings by Manet and Renoir, *The Rehearsal* is one of twenty works by Hilaire-Germain-Edgar Degas *52* that explore the subject of young ballet dancers practicing in the classroom. Accompanied by an aged violinist, whose bulbous nose and sausage-like fingers contrast with the gracefulness of the spectacle depicted, four young ballerinas are engaged in their center floor exercises, raising their legs in a *battement* or *développé à la seconde*, a standard element of their daily training. We see three of the dancers completely; the fourth is represented only by her tutu and pink slipper at the right-hand edge of the composition. Despite the actuality of the scene, it is likely that Degas showed his ballerinas in the classroom of the old Opera House on the rue Le Peletier that had burned down in 1873. This large room, measuring thirty by twenty-five feet, had high ceilings and a central group of three tall windows overlooking an interior courtyard. Exhibited at the Fourth Impressionist exhibition in 1879 as "École de Danse," Degas's *Rehearsal* was in all likelihood elaborated over many years. Several preparatory drawings have been identified, and it is clear that this seemingly spontaneous composition was crafted with the greatest care and forethought, Degas working both from life studies and from memory, and modifying, correcting, and revising his image even as he painted it.

British Paintings

Like works by northern artists, British paintings were eagerly sought by the wealthiest American collectors in the nineteenth and early twentieth centuries. Grand images of dignified sitters and idyllic landscapes adorned American millionaires' mansions as they formerly had the country estates of the British aristocracy.

Of the many British portraits in The Frick Collection there is perhaps none that is more dramatic in its subject's lavish appearance and biography than *Miss Mary Edwards*. Purchased by Frick in 1914, it was painted in 1742 by *53* Edwards's friend the painter and engraver William Hogarth. Mary's pleasing face and affable expression are easily overlooked in favor of the voluminous

53. William Hogarth (1697–1764),
Miss Mary Edwards, 1742, oil on
canvas, 49 ¾ x 39 ⅞ (126.4 x 101.3)

1914.1.75

scarlet sack-back gown, her parure of diamonds, pearl necklace, rings, gold chatelaine, and watch. Delicate brushstrokes describe the Belgian lace embellishing her cap, décolletage, and sleeves. Behind her is a globe suggesting worldliness, while busts of Elizabeth I and Alfred the Great—illustrious defenders of the English realm—confirm her patriotism. On the table, an unfurled scroll excerpts a text from Joseph Addison's play *Cato* praising individual liberty. On her father's death, twenty-four-year-old Mary Edwards had come into his fortune, making her one of the richest women in England. Soon after, she secretly wed the Scotsman Lord Anne Hamilton (1709–1748), with whom she had a son, Gerard Anne Edwards (1733–1773). Rumored infidelities and Lord Hamilton's profligate spending reportedly led Mary to have the records of her marriage destroyed, effectively rendering her son illegitimate. This bold

54. Joshua Reynolds (1723–1792), *General John Burgoyne*, c. 1766, oil on canvas, 50 x 39 ⅞ (127 x 101.3)
1943.1.149

move protected her fortune. Mindful of the need to safeguard her wealth, she drafted her will the year this portrait was made; her foresight was admirable, since she died the following year at the age of thirty-eight.

Sir Joshua Reynolds was the leading portraitist of the eighteenth century. Inspired by ancient art and the Italian masters, Reynolds created memorable images imbued with intellectual and historic references. A friend of General John Burgoyne (1722–1792), known as "Gentleman Johnny," Reynolds in all likelihood was commissioned to paint this portrait by Wilhelm, count of Schaumburg-Lippe Bückeburg (1724–1777), Burgoyne's commanding officer during the Seven Years' War. Posed atop a precipice in his dashing uniform of the Sixteenth Light Dragoons, the heroic Burgoyne emerges from the smoky chaos of combat, genteel and poised in his striking red coat. Below, a battle surges against the blurred outlines of Valencia de Alcántara, the Spanish town captured by Burgoyne's troops. Admiration for the commander's martial prowess declined after his surrender to American troops at Saratoga in 1777. His ornate sword may be the one relinquished to General Horatio Gates (1727–1806) following this defeat. Aside from his military career, Burgoyne was a member of fashionable society after his elopement with Lady Charlotte Stanley, daughter of the Earl of Derby. He was also an actor, popular playwright, and Member of Parliament.

Reynolds's classical approach was somewhat at odds with that of his fellow artist Thomas Gainsborough, who valued nature's inspiration as much as the influence of the Old Masters. Gainsborough's spontaneous handling of paint was perplexing to the methodical Reynolds, who, after reconciling with his dying colleague, acknowledged his rival's achievements as "a kind of magic."

Gainsborough's *Mall in St. James's Park*, probably painted in 1783, exhibits this "magic" described by Reynolds. In a landscape overflowing with downy foliage, cows, and dogs reminiscent of Watteau's *fêtes galantes* stride groups of fashionably attired ladies, some escorted by equally well-appointed gentlemen. All gather to take in the fresh air and sunshine—and one another—in a scene loosely based on observations of the public promenading in St. James's Park, located near Gainsborough's London residence. Some accounts claim that the group of ethereal ladies at center represents the daughters of George III, but this seems unlikely. Similarly, assertions that the artist included himself sketching under a tree in the background at right are unproven. Gainsborough may have used dolls and model landscapes to assist him in the elaboration of his Watteauesque composition. With his pulsating colors and flickering brush-strokes, Gainsborough has created a modern equivalent of a Garden of Love.

John Constable yearned to be an Academician. *The White Horse*, purchased by the Collection in 1943, was the first of Constable's "six-footer" paintings. Depicting views of his native Suffolk, the oversized canvases demanded notice from Academicians and the public alike and elevated these modest, bucolic images to the level of history painting. The child of a mill owner, Constable was intimately familiar with life on the Stour River. His scene depicts a tow-horse being transported across the waterway below Flatford Lock to the towpath on the opposite bank. Populated with cottages, a thatched boatshed, a barn, and cows, the verdant countryside awakens and the languid river iridesces beneath a morning sky in summer. Although a practitioner of plein-air sketching, Constable composed this canvas in his London studio with the assistance of numerous preparatory works, including one in oil of identical scale. While he

55

56

56. John Constable (1776–1837),
The White Horse, 1819, oil on canvas,
51 ¾ x 74 ⅛ (131.4 x 188.3)
1943.1.147

favored the vigor of Gainsborough's irregular brushstrokes, Constable modified his technique somewhat in deference to the Academy's preference for more finished pictures. *The White Horse* was well received at the 1819 exhibition and ensured his election as an Associate. Before the exhibition's close it was purchased by the artist's good friend Archdeacon John Fisher. Constable would buy the painting—one of his personal favorites—back from Fisher in 1829 after a reversal in the latter's fortunes. Calling it "one of my happiest efforts on a large scale," Constable kept it in his studio until his death.

While Constable found inspiration in the familiar countryside of eastern England, Joseph Mallord William Turner, largely self-trained as a topographical draftsman and painter, ventured across Europe in addition to exploring his native land. *The Harbor of Dieppe* evolved from a series of sketches made by Turner during a visit to France in the summer of 1821. In 1825 the monumental canvas was exhibited at the Royal Academy in London, where he was already a member. Although the painting's brilliant composition was lauded, detractors found the intense illumination unrealistic. In his majestic scene, identifiable landmarks—like the bustling Quai Henri IV, the grand Hôtel d'Anvers, the Collège Communal at right, and the blurred cupola of St.-Jacques in the distance at left—encircle the serene harbor filled to capacity with ships. But it is the light, its blazing image reflected across the tranquil water's surface, that colors the scene in tones of cream, russet, and amber and elevates the picture from a topographical rendering to an enduring classical landscape. Frick purchased *Dieppe* in 1914 along with another beautiful picture of a continental port by the artist, *Cologne: The Arrival of a Packet-Boat: Evening*, which had been exhibited at the Academy in 1826.

Prompted by laments that the high color of *Cologne* detracted from two portraits by Sir Thomas Lawrence installed next to the mammoth canvas, Turner is said to have dimmed his painting's resplendent sky with lampblack. Surely this measure would have been unnecessary had one of the Lawrence paintings been his bold portrait of *Julia, Lady Peel*. Born in India, Julia Floyd Peel (1795—1859) was the daughter of General Sir John Floyd, a British army officer. In 1820 she married and later had seven children by the British Conservative statesman Sir Robert Peel (1788–1850). An advocate of social reform, Peel would serve twice as Britain's prime minister. Also an art collector, he commissioned Lawrence to paint his wife's portrait on two occasions, and the Frick picture was exhibited at the Royal Academy in 1827 to great acclaim. Lady Peel is festooned in an array of liquid satin, downy feathers, and sparkling gems. Lawrence represents these sumptuous textures by juxtaposing fields of carefully blended, smooth brushstrokes with freer passages, formed by irregular strokes and impastoed surfaces. Peel's glossy brunette hair is tucked under her broad black hat, from which a torrent of red feathers forms a veil of plumage. Lady Peel's pose and elaborate headdress derive from Peter Paul Rubens's celebrated *Chapeau de Paille* (The National Gallery, London), a portrait of his future sister-in-law painted in the early 1620s, which Peel had acquired in 1823.

James Abbott McNeill Whistler also immortalized a prominent patron's wife in oil. Born in Lowell, Massachusetts, he was active in France and England, moving to London in 1859 and remaining there for most of his life. Just as Lawrence conjured Lady Peel's whimsical costume for maximum visual impact, so Whistler selected his sitters' attire to create harmonious and calculated images. Frances Dawson (1834–1910) was married to Frederick R. Leyland (1831–1892), a wealthy Liverpool shipowner and one of Whistler's principal patrons. For *Symphony in Flesh Colour and Pink: Portrait of Mrs. Frances Leyland*, painted between 1871 and 1874, Whistler designed Mrs. Leyland's chiffon tea

gown, with its cascading gossamer train, attempting it in numerous preliminary sketches. He then translated the sensuous fabric into oil paint using long, fluid strokes. He devised the room's interior—its pink walls, white dado, and rush rug—to complement the tones of his subject's gown, while asymmetrically positioned almond blossoms inject a note of *japonisme*. Mrs. Leyland's profile is recognizable but somewhat indistinct, her portrait simply another element of Whistler's overall design. As the work's title suggests, Whistler was intent on creating tonal harmonies, declaring, "As music is the poetry of sound, so is painting the poetry of sight." He would repaint the portrait repeatedly and never considered it finished. Frick purchased the painting in 1916, one of five works by the artist that he would acquire.

57. Joseph Mallord William Turner (1775–1851), *The Harbor of Dieppe*, 1825–26, oil on canvas, 68 ⅜ x 88 ¾ (173.7 x 225.4)
1914.1.122

58. Sir Thomas Lawrence (1769–1830),
Julia, Lady Peel, 1827, oil on canvas,
35 ¾ x 27 ⅞ (90.8 x 70.8)
1904.1.83

59. James Abbott McNeill Whistler
(1834–1903), *Symphony in Flesh Colour
and Pink: Portrait of Mrs. Frances
Leyland*, 1871–74, oil on canvas,
77 ⅛ x 40 ¼ (195.9 x 102.2)
1916.1.133

Sculpture

In 1915, after moving into the mansion at 1 East 70th Street, Henry Clay Frick turned his attention to sculpture. He began acquiring bronzes to embellish the interiors of his home and to complement his paintings. An ink holder then attributed to Riccio and the imposing *Hercules and the Hydra* were placed in the Library, while the magnificent *Nessus and Deianira* became the centerpiece of the Picture Gallery. Frick lived with these works for at least a year before making his most significant sculpture acquisition in 1916: eighty-six of the financier J. P. Morgan's renowned Renaissance bronzes, described by the German art historian and museum director Wilhelm von Bode as "probably the most important collection of bronzes to be found in private possession."

Frick had the Morgan bronzes arranged in the Picture Gallery, the Library, and the Living Hall, where Severo da Ravenna's *Neptune on a Sea-Monster* took center stage. The largest, most dramatic Morgan sculptures commanded attention from all sides on three long tables at the center of the Picture Gallery. Finely detailed lamps and inkstands—objects originally made for Renaissance scholars' studies—found fitting places on top of the Library's bookcases. The sculptures introduced mythological and religious themes into Frick's art collection, where portraits and landscapes had predominated. The small-scale bronze figures, which were often expressive nudes, complemented his paintings' more restrained subjects. Yet in acquiring sculpture Frick also indulged his taste for portraits of distinguished men and beautiful women. In March 1916 Frick purchased Jean-Antoine Houdon's late eighteenth-century marble portrait of the sylphlike *Comtesse du Cayla*. He also purchased four Renaissance portrait busts, including the serene marble *Bust of a Lady*, attributed to Francesco Laurana, and three male bronze busts by Jonghelinck, Brandani, and Cattaneo. Frick had purchased these busts to anchor the corners of his Picture Gallery, and in 1918 they were joined by his last sculpture acquisition, Antoine Coysevox's bronze *Henri de la Tour d'Auvergne, Maréchal Turenne*.

After her father's death in 1919, Helen Clay Frick continued his interest in sculpture. As a self-trained Houdon specialist, she advocated for the acquisition of the *Marquis de Miromesnil* in 1935 and Houdon's virtuosic life-size terracotta *Diana* in 1939. Building on Frick's appreciation for portrait busts, the trustees purchased a second bronze bust by Coysevox in 1945 and received, through the bequest of John D. Rockefeller, Jr., two marble Renaissance busts by Laurana and Verrocchio. The Collection's fine holdings of Severo da Ravenna's and Houdon's sculpture have been augmented by recent gifts. Seventeenth- and eighteenth-century Italian sculpture was not well represented in Frick's collection, and this area has been strengthened in the last twenty years thanks to gifts of works by Giovanni Francesco Susini and Massimiliano Soldani-Benzi.

60. Attributed to Pietro Tacca (1577–1640), *Nessus and Deianira*, early 17th century. Detail of ill. 70

Renaissance Bronzes

In the summer of 1916 Frick bought from Joseph Duveen the early Renaissance relief of *The Resurrection* by the Sienese master Lorenzo Vecchietta. *The Resurrection* is signed and dated with the year 1472. An artist of great technical agility, Vecchietta worked as a painter, architect, and sculptor of wood before turning to bronze in the later part of his career. His interest may have been kindled by Donatello's work on bronze doors for the Siena cathedral between 1457 and 1459. Donatello's influence is evident in the extremely low-relief putti playing in the clouds, which recall the Florentine sculptor's characteristic *schiacciato* technique. A variety of functions have been proposed for this relief, but its original application remains unknown. Vecchietta cast it in one pour, neatly capturing details like the angels' feathered wings and the soldiers' elaborate Roman armor.

The relief's central focus is Christ's resurrected body, floating in a nimbus of seraphim. Vecchietta evokes Christ's humanity within this image of divinity, showing the skin of his chest and shoulders pulled tightly across the bone. The scale is hieratic: Christ, as the protagonist, is larger and more robustly modeled than any other figure. Vecchietta's adherence to this convention for organizing figural relationships contrasts with the concern for perspectival effects evident in his bold foreshortening of the sarcophagus lid and the sleeping soldiers. The artist doubtless drew on his experience as a painter to bring these disparate elements together in a work of remarkable compositional harmony.

Bertoldo di Giovanni may have begun creating small-scale bronze statues of mythological figures perhaps even before the 1470s, not long after he left Donatello's employ. He also produced several medals for Lorenzo de' Medici in this decade and came to be part of the Florentine ruler's household. Bertoldo's familiarity with Lorenzo's sophisticated circle and his knowledge of antiquities enabled him to create classicizing statuettes, reliefs, and medals that appealed to his patrons' sophisticated tastes.

The *Heraldic Wild Man* (1470–75) carries a club and wears a wreath and a sash of vine, attributes that connect him to both Hercules and Bacchus. However, the figure's horns and tufted tail identify him as a faun. By gilding the bronze surface, Bertoldo imbued the work with preciousness and evokes the magnificence of ancient bronze sculpture. A pendant statuette that mirrors the Frick version in almost every detail exists in the Liechtenstein collection in Vaduz.

Northern Italian courts like Mantua were centers for the production of small bronzes at the turn of the sixteenth century. The Gonzaga princes envisioned Mantua as a "new Rome," and under their patronage Pier Jacopo Alari Bonacolsi produced richly embellished statuettes that evoke the splendor of antiquity. Bonacolsi worked as a sculptor and restorer of antiquities at the Gonzaga court for almost his entire career, ultimately succeeding Mantegna as Isabella d'Este's artistic adviser in 1506. He was nicknamed "Antico" for his ability to interpret ancient sources and emulate classical forms. Antico was capable of producing multiple versions of his compositions by using piece molds that allowed him to save his original wax models for repeated use. Statuettes made from the same wax model could be altered in finish and detail according to the demands of different commissions.

The finest of the five extant versions of Antico's *Hercules* is the Frick bronze, which has gilded hair and lion skin and silvered eyes that contrast brilliantly with the darkly patinated metal. Letters in the spring of 1499 from Antico's patron Bishop Ludovico Gonzaga record the bishop's attempts to hurry the delivery of *Hercules* as the artist was apparently lingering over its chasing. Antico's training as a goldsmith is revealed in the exquisite tooling of

61. Lorenzo di Pietro di Giovanni (Vecchietta) (1410–80), *The Resurrection*, 1472, bronze, 21 3/8 x 16 1/4 (54.3 x 41.3)
1916.2.02

VECCHIETTA
THE RESURRECTION

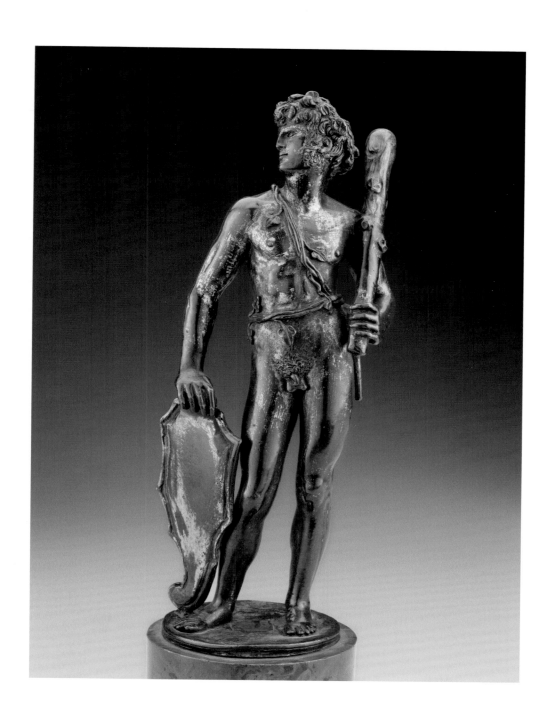

62. Pier Jacopo Alari Bonacolsi
(Antico) (c. 1460–1528), *Hercules*,
c. 1499, bronze with gilding, and silver
inlay, on bronze base, 13 ⅝ high (34.6)

Gift of Miss Helen Clay Frick, 1970. 1970.2.89

63. Bertoldo di Giovanni (1420/30–1491),
Heraldic Wild Man, early 1470s,
bronze with extensive traces of
gilding, on base, 8 ¹⁵⁄₁₆ high (22.4)

1916.2.03

81

the bronze surface: a multitude of tiny incised lines mimic the natural swirls of hair in the lion's skin, and each lock of Hercules' hair and beard is deeply chiseled to achieve a bold, rippled texture.

Naked Female Figure is one of the many Renaissance bronzes that defy 64 easy attribution. The modeling of the torso is sensuous and fluent, and the refinement of certain details—such as the fingertips, bared teeth, and intricate coiffure—suggest that the artist was trained as a goldsmith. Once ascribed to Andrea Riccio, the work displays a dependence on an antique prototype that more closely relates it to statuettes produced at this time in Mantua by Antico. The figure's expression of outrage recalls impassioned characters in Mantegna's paintings, further linking the bronze to a Mantuan context.

The sculpture's subject is a matter of debate. A nude woman is depicted in a fugitive, momentary pose, struggling to preserve her modesty while reacting angrily to a provocation. Although the figure is sometimes thought to be Eve or the biblical heroine Susanna surprised at her bath, the ferocity of her expression argues instead for her identification as Diana seen bathing by Actaeon. The Venus Pudica pose clearly derives from an ancient torso, like that of the *Medici Venus*, and the eyes and nipples are inlaid in silver in emulation of a Greek bronze. Such classicizing accents would have been more appropriate for a mythological subject than a biblical one. As one of the earliest

65. Riccio (Andrea Briosco) (1470–1532), *Lamp*, c. 1516–24, bronze, 6 ⅝ high (16.8)
1916.2.18

64. Mantuan (?), *Naked Female Figure*, early 16th century, bronze, 10 ½ high (26.7)
1916.2.14

independent statuettes with an implied narrative, this work anticipates the growing complexity and inventiveness of sixteenth-century bronze sculpture.

Padua was a center for humanist studies in the Renaissance. Patricians from Venice were educated at its distinguished university, which also attracted eminent scholars from across the Continent. Bronze sculpture had been accorded special prominence in Padua since Donatello's residence of 1443–53, and the city's erudite elite held in high esteem masters of the medium like Andrea Riccio.

Renaissance scholars were aware of ancient bronze prototypes for functional items like oil lamps and inkwells, and they commissioned such objects for use in their private studies. One of four lamps attributed to Riccio, the Frick *Lamp* demonstrates the sculptor's ability to realize in bronze his patrons' ideas about the classical past. This lamp, now missing its lid, held oil in its oval well and would have offered light from its spout. The flickering flame would have appeared to animate the long tendrils curling around the lamp's body. Each vine emerges from a grotesque mask or winged harpy, fantastic hybrid creatures that were Renaissance emblems of creativity. *65*

Riccio modeled each minute figure directly in the wax. The cast preserved the movement of his hand, requiring little afterwork to make the decoration legible. He designed the lamp to stand independently, balancing its long, heavy body on a delicate socle supported by four tiny feet. For an erudite Paduan scholar—like the probable patron of this work—the *Lamp*'s inventive form and complex imagery would have rewarded countless viewings.

Both Riccio and his contemporary Severo da Ravenna are praised by the humanist Pomponio Gaurico in his 1504 treatise *De Sculptura*. Severo appears to have worked in Padua in the first decade of the sixteenth century before returning by 1511 to his native Ravenna, where he opened a hugely successful workshop. Few of the works associated with his shop attain the level of expression and execution of the Frick's *Neptune on a Sea-Monster* and *Sea-Monster*. *66, 67*

Neptune on a Sea-Monster is one of Severo's most ambitious figural compositions. Neptune is depicted as master of the seas, raising his trident aloft as he stands on the scaly back of a sea-monster. The god looks sternly on the gaping maw, which is wonderfully detailed with two rows of sharp teeth and a giant flapping tongue. The reins with which Neptune restrained this fantastic beast

66. Severo da Ravenna (Severo Calzetta) (1465/75–before 1538), *Neptune on a Sea-Monster*, c. 1510, bronze, 13 ⅜ x 11 ½ (34 x 29.2)
1916.2.12

67. Severo da Ravenna (Severo Calzetta) (1465/75–before 1538), *Sea-Monster*, c. 1510, bronze, 4 ½ x 9 ¾ (11.4 x 24.8)
Gift of Eugene and Clare Thaw in honor of Charles Ryskamp, Director of The Frick Collection, and in memory of Ruth Blumka, 1997. 1997.2.103

are missing. This motif proved to be popular, and the figures of the god and monster exist in multiple versions (and often in isolation).

The Frick *Sea-Monster* represents the adaptation of the creature-model for use as an inkstand. Here, the monster's face takes on a half-human, half-vegetal appearance, and the figure of Neptune has been replaced by the shell-shaped inkwell. When this element is removed, the collar of the attachment-hole displays the inscription .O.SEVERI.RA. This signature matches that of a marble statue of St. John the Baptist executed by Severo in Padua in 1500. The discovery of this signature occasioned the reattribution of the entire group of Neptune and Sea-Monster bronzes to Severo da Ravenna.

The Frick *Neptune on a Sea-Monster* and *Sea-Monster* stand out among the numerous statuettes attributed to Severo because of the quality of their execution. Neither bronze shows much evidence of tooling to reinforce the textures and expressions of these extraordinarily vibrant compositions. Most of the definition is "in the wax"—that is, expressed in the modeling stage and crisply preserved through the difficult casting process.

Renaissance Portrait Busts

Frick's taste for Renaissance sculpture encompassed both bronzes and portrait busts. In 1916 he purchased an elegant marble bust of a lady attributed to Francesco Laurana, and in 1961 the bequest of John D. Rockefeller, Jr., brought
69 Laurana's *Beatrice of Aragon* to the collection.

The surname "Laurana" derives from "La Vrana," the name of the sculptor's hometown in Dalmatia. Laurana's career was peripatetic: he is known to have worked in Sicily, Naples, and southern France, and his presence has also been hypothesized in Genoa, Rimini, and Urbino. He is best known for his enigmatic female portrait busts, which are characterized by an almost geometric perfection of form. None of the nine portrait busts traditionally ascribed to Laurana is signed, dated, or documented. One of only two busts with inscriptions identifying their sitters, *Beatrice* is the sole work for which a date can plausibly be advanced: between 1471 and 1474.

The daughter of Ferdinand I, king of Naples, Beatrice (1457–1508) married the king of Hungary, Matthias Corvinus, by proxy in 1476. Her portrait was probably commissioned before the marriage as a likeness to send to the prospective bridegroom. This was a common practice among Renaissance courts and may have been particularly relevant in this case as Matthias had previously rejected Beatrice's older sister's hand, declaring that he wanted "una bellissima" for a wife. In Laurana's portrait Beatrice appears fresh faced, with full, smooth cheeks and a slightly impish nose. In keeping with the ideals of courtly decorum, her eyes are modestly downcast. The sculptor carefully rendered the wisps of hair that escape from her cap and the texture of her light tunic. Traces of colored pigment were found in the recesses of her tunic's borders, and it is possible that this bust—like another portrait by Laurana in Vienna—was once selectively polychromed. Though Beatrice was just a girl at the time, her portrait conveys the composure that sustained her in Hungary, where her involvement in affairs of state was frustrated by her failure to produce an heir.

Frick acquired four bronze Renaissance busts, the finest of which is Jacques
68 Jonghelinck's *Duke of Alba*. Born in Antwerp, Jonghelinck visited Italy in 1552 and may have worked in the Milanese studio of Leone Leoni. He returned to Flanders by 1555 and was appointed official sculptor, metal-caster, and seal-engraver to Philip II in 1556.

Don Fernando Alvarez de Toledo (1507–1582), the third Duke of Alba, successfully commanded Spanish forces at the siege of Tunis (1535) and the

68. Jacques Jonghelinck (1530–1606), *The Duke of Alba*, 1571, bronze, 45 ⅞ (116.5)
1916.2.61

69. Francesco Laurana (c.1430–c.1502), *Beatrice of Aragon*, 1471–74, white marble, 16 x 15 ⅞ x 8 (40.6 x 40.3 x 20.3)
Bequest of John D. Rockefeller, Jr., 1961. 1961.2.86

battle of Mühlberg (1547). The Catholic monarch Philip II appointed him governor-general of the Protestant Low Countries in 1567. His tenure in the Netherlands was marked by severe religious intolerance and the pitiless suppression of civil opposition. His tyranny ultimately forced the king to recall him to Spain in 1573.

Jonghelinck was commissioned to portray Alba in two medals, a full-length statue, and the present bust. The sculptor rendered the sitter's armor, sash, and decoration—the Order of the Golden Fleece—in the painstaking detail appropriate to an official portrait. With his probing stare and formidable expression, Alba appears the epitome of military hauteur. Jonghelinck's success in capturing the leader's fearsome persona may have led, in part, to the destruction of his full-length statue in Antwerp. The next governor-general ordered the work dismantled and buried in 1574 and destroyed in 1577. The statue's burial was commemorated in a medal by Jonghelinck, which showed the Fall of Icarus on the reverse. Jonghelinck's bust accompanied Alba back to Spain, where it remained with his descendants until 1810.

Late Sixteenth- and Seventeenth-Century Bronzes

Born Jean Boulogne, in French Flanders, Giambologna (1529–1608) settled in Florence in 1553. He became the official sculptor to the Medici and earned an international reputation for executing sculptures of tremendous complexity and sophistication. Giambologna relied on a workshop of talented assistants to reproduce his designs. Those who inherited his studio continued to cast works from his molds, giving rise to notable problems of attribution.

One of Giambologna's most famous compositions, *Nessus and Deianira* exists in multiple versions that vary in size and in detail. The first documented group was made in Florence between 1575 and 1577. The Frick work is one of the largest examples. The collector acquired it in 1915 as a work by Adriaen de Vries (1556?–1626), a northern sculptor who trained with Giambologna. It has since been reattributed to Pietro Tacca, who followed his master in the role of court sculptor to the Medici grand dukes.

Nessus attempted to abduct Deianira, the wife of Hercules, after offering to carry her over a river on his back. Hercules saved his wife by slaying the centaur with an arrow. Giambologna chose to represent the moment of Nessus's flight, contrasting Deianira's terror with his ferocious determination. Only by circling the sculpture and viewing it from all sides can one grasp the full drama of their confrontation. The composition's wild energy becomes even more audacious in Tacca's cast, which tests the tensile strength of bronze with Nessus's high rearing pose and intensifies the subject's inherent violence. The near flawlessness of the cast—which reveals every straining muscle and vein—testifies to Tacca's technical brilliance, which equaled that of his master.

The Florentine sculptor Giovanni Francesco Susini trained on Giambologna's models in the studio of his uncle Antonio, who had been the master's principal bronze caster. The pendant bronzes *A Lion Attacking a Horse* and *A Leopard Attacking a Bull* represent the younger Susini's interpretation of the subject of animals in combat, an antique theme reinvented by Giambologna around 1580. Probably cast between 1630 and 1640, they depict predatory cats striking their prey. The lion group derives from a model by Antonio Susini, while *Leopard Attacking a Bull* is Giovanni's own invention.

Though locked in conflict, the lion and horse relate gracefully to each other, forming a harmonious composition characteristic of Giovanni's sixteenth-century predecessors. Their battle, it seems, could go on forever.

70

71, 72

70. Attributed to Pietro Tacca (1577–1640), *Nessus and Deianira*, early 17th century, bronze, 34¾ high (88.2) 1915.2.49

71. Giovanni Francesco Susini
(1585–after 1653), *A Lion Attacking a
Horse*, c. 1630–40, bronze, 9 ½ x 11 ¾
(24.2 x 30)

Gift of Walter A. and Vera Eberstadt, 2002. 2002.2.02

72. Giovanni Francesco Susini
(1585–after 1653), *A Leopard Attacking
a Bull*, c. 1630–40, bronze, 4 ¾ x 10 ¾
(11.9 x 27.5)

Gift of Walter A. and Vera Eberstadt, 2002. 2002.2.03

73. *Hercules and the Hydra*, France,
mid-17th century, bronze,
22 ⅜ high (56.8)

1915.2.53

The bull, in contrast, falls heavily to his knees, having already lost the fight. The apparent suddenness and savagery of the leopard's attack is reinforced by the angularity of the composition. Powerful anatomical details, such as the claw marks sunk deep into the victims' flesh, bring us closer to each animal's struggle. Susini worked the bronze surface extensively after casting, using small chisels to articulate details like the animals' pupils and the leopard's spots. Only two pairs of Giovanni's lion and horse and leopard and bull pendants survive. The second group went directly from the artist's studio to the collection of the prince of Liechtenstein, where it remains today.

Tacca and Susini were among the last sculptors formed in the brilliant intellectual milieu of sixteenth-century Florence, and their work enjoyed great success among the rarefied courts of Europe. A number of sculptors outside of Italy emulated this virtuosic late Renaissance style to great effect, and, as a result, many of their works later carried erroneous attributions to Giambologna or his assistants. The *Hercules and the Hydra* is a case in point: purchased by Frick in 1915 as a work by Giambologna, it is now considered the masterpiece of an as yet unknown French master.

Defeating the vicious hydra was one of Hercules' twelve labors. In the Frick bronze, Hercules prepares to club the many heads of the beast swarming around his right leg, having already subdued one by grasping its neck. Light ripples over the hydra's sinuous forms and Hercules' powerful torso, animating their battle. The artist conjured up the fantastic creature using attributes recognizable from more mundane animals, such as an ox, serpent, hawk, and hound.

This bronze may be connected to a *Hercules and the Hydra* by Giambologna documented in 1580/81. However, the finely detailed head of the Frick Hercules is distinct from every other related work. The suggestion that the figure bears the features of Henri IV of France is supported by comparison with portraits of the king. According to legend, Henri IV's House of Navarre descended from Hercules' son Hispalus, whom he established as king of Navarre, one of the many kingdoms of Spain, during the completion of his labors. This dynastic myth intersects with the tradition of the Gallic Hercules, in whom noble virtues complement martial ability. Late sixteenth-century representations of Henri IV as the laboring Hercules partake of both traditions and may allude to the ruler's struggles against the Catholic League.

Eighteenth-Century Sculpture

Massimiliano Soldani-Benzi began his career under the patronage of Duke Cosimo III, who intended him for the Florentine mint. He was sent to Rome in 1678 and thence to Paris in 1682. His large-format portrait medal of Louis XIV led to an offer to enter the king's service, but Soldani returned to Florence instead, where he oversaw a large workshop that produced figural sculpture, reliefs, and portrait busts in addition to coins and medals.

Soldani's tender *Pietà with Two Mourning Putti* owes much to his experience copying models by Alessandro Algardi (c. 1595–1654) in Rome. Made in 1715 for use during private religious devotions, it is the only known example of this composition. A pair of angels grieves before Christ's dead body, helping to guide the viewer's response to his sacrifice. One leans down to kiss Christ's hand, drawing attention to his wound, while the second gazes sorrowfully into his unseeing eyes. Despite the insults to his body, Soldani's Christ is compellingly beautiful. His sensuously modeled figure appears more languorous than lifeless. Soldani's graceful rendering tempers the somber subject, suggesting that in Christ's death lies the promise of resurrection and eternal life.

74. Claude Michel Clodion (1738–1814), *Zephyrus and Flora*, 1799, terracotta, 20 ¾ high (52.7)

1915.2.76

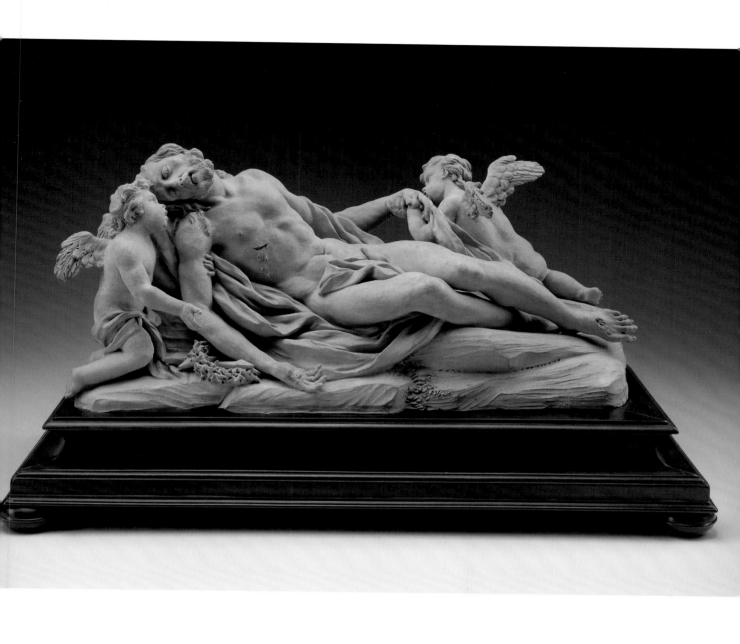

75. Massimiliano Soldani-Benzi
(1656–1740), *Pietà with Two Mourning
Putti*, 1715, terracotta on ebony base,
11 ⅝ x 21 ⅝ (29.5 x 54.9)

Gift of The Quentin Foundation, 2006. 2006.2.03

Some of Soldani's rare terracotta groups survived because the sculptor made gifts of them to esteemed patrons. At the time collectors were beginning to value sketches and models as the purest expressions of artistic creativity. A finished terracotta model by Soldani would have been a true prize for such connoisseurs. His ability to make the clay follow his intentions is extraordinary—one is utterly convinced by details like the spiky crown of thorns, the blood thickening in Christ's wounds, and the angels' feathered wings. Though Soldani is today considered Florence's last great bronze sculptor—concluding a tradition that goes back to the fourteenth century—his relationship to the nascent eighteenth-century revival of terracotta sculpture as an independent art form should also be recognized.

During his Parisian sojourn Soldani entered the orbit of Antoine Coysevox, the premier portrait sculptor at the court of Louis XIV. In this official role, Coysevox executed a series of busts and equestrian portraits of the Sun King, as well as monumental and decorative sculpture. He also fulfilled private commissions for portraits of many of the court's most illustrious members, including Jean-Baptiste Colbert and Charles Le Brun.

Coysevox's talent for capturing a sitter's personality is amply demonstrated by the bust of the distinguished architect Robert de Cotte (1656–1735), a friend *76* and colleague. Clearly modeled from life, the portrait captures the energy and determination of a man in middle age. The expression on De Cotte's lightly lined face is open but serious, his eyes alert and searching. Coysevox's technical mastery is evident in each flawlessly cast curl of the sitter's luxuriant peruke. Two other versions of this portrait survive, one in marble, dated 1707, and one in plaster. Coysevox exhibited a bust of De Cotte in the Salon of 1704. Though the material for that bust is not given, this suggests that the Frick bust dates from the first years of the eighteenth century.

The Enlightenment sculptor Jean-Antoine Houdon left a similarly brilliant gallery of leading figures of the day. The Salon of 1775 marked his emergence as one of the great portraitists of his age. Then a candidate for full membership in the Academy, Houdon exhibited an exceptional array of portraits, including the marble busts of Madame His, née Marie-Anne Damaris Dumoustier *77* de Vastre, and Armand-Thomas Hue, Marquis de Miromesnil (now in the Victoria & Albert Museum, London). A second bust of Miromesnil (1723–1796) *78* was executed in 1777 and acquired by the Frick in 1935. Created in the same incandescent moment, these two works illuminate the range and depth of Houdon's formidable talent.

The attractive wife of a German banker, Madame His appears to have been on close terms with Houdon and his wife. Madame His's expression of bright composure is achieved through the subtle modeling of her face, the faint parting of the lips, and the remarkable penetration of her gaze. Her warm, intelligent eyes are carved in a manner that is characteristic of Houdon's portraits. After drilling a hole for the pupil, the artist added a small circle of marble that catches the light and suggests a sparkling glance. To show the texture of her upswept hair Houdon finely scored the marble above her forehead. The curls piled high on her head in the fashion of the 1770s cascade down her back, with a few tendrils falling on her nude shoulder. Houdon presents his sitter in a shoulder-baring chemise and a cloak secured by a diagonal band. This strap recalls antique depictions of Diana the Huntress carrying a quiver of arrows over her shoulder. The artist may have adopted the costume and format of this portrait from Augustin Pajou's bust of Madame du Barry, which had been exhibited at the Salon of 1773.

Houdon's facility with marble is nowhere more evident than in the *Marquis de Miromesnil*'s exquisitely preserved surface. Every texture, from the

76. Antoine Coysevox (1640–1720), *Robert de Cotte*, early 18th century, bronze, 21 ⅜ high (54.29)
Purchased by The Frick Collection, 1945. 1945.2.83

77. Jean-Antoine Houdon
(1741–1828), *Madame His*, 1775, marble,
31 ½ x 17 x 12 ½ (80.01 x 43.2 x 31.8)

Gift of Mr. and Mrs. Eugene Victor Thaw, 2007.
2007.2.01

78. Jean-Antoine Houdon (1741–1828),
*Armand-Thomas Hue, Marquis
de Miromesnil*, 1777, marble,
25 ½ high (64.8)

Purchased by The Frick Collection, 1935. 1935.2.78

79. Claude Michel Clodion (1738–1814), sculptor, Jean-Baptiste Lepaute (1727–1802), clockmaker, *The Dance of Time, Three Nymphs Supporting a Clock*, 1788, terracotta, 40 ¾ high (103.5)

Purchased by The Frick Collection through the Winthrop Kellogg Edey Bequest, 2006. 2006.2.02

heavily lidded eyes to the pleated sleeves and broad sash, is palpably distinct. Represented in an enormous powdered wig and stiff, heavy robes, Miromesnil evinces the dignity and immutability of his position as minister of justice. His expression, however, appears fleeting, and his raised eyebrows and slightly sidelong glance reveal an active mind and a thoughtful nature.

This portrait may have been commissioned to commemorate Miromesnil's appointment as minister by Louis XVI in 1774. He was forced to relinquish this role in 1787. An inscription on the back of the bust—A. T. HUE ... DE MIROMENIL. FAIT PAR HOUDON EN 1777—indicates that his title was effaced, probably during the Revolution.

Houdon's contemporary Claude Michel Clodion reinvented the terracotta statuette in the second half of the eighteenth century. During a nine-year stay in Rome (1762–71), he studied antique sculpture and contemporary art, conceiving the harmony of classical and baroque grace that would define his greatest works. The Frick Collection owns two superlative examples of his mature sculpture, *The Dance of Time, Three Nymphs Supporting a Clock* and *Zephyrus and Flora*.

The Dance of Time (1788) is a rare eighteenth-century clock that features a sculpture in terracotta. A collaboration between Clodion and the horologist Jean-Baptiste Lepaute, it presents three semi-draped nymphs dancing around a column supporting a gilt-brass pendulum clock with a rotating annual dial. Clodion's figures may represent the three Horae (hours), who personify the passage of time in Greek mythology. With this work Lepaute introduced the transparent glass globe, which reveals the clock's motion. Its mechanical revolution is echoed by the nymphs' circular dance, uniting the classicizing figures under a symbol of the mathematically ordered cosmos. Fashioned on the eve of the Revolution, this brilliant marriage of art and science is a masterpiece of both the sculptor's and the clockmaker's art. Clodion and Lepaute created this work for the well-known architect Alexandre-Théodore Brongniart, who was its first owner. The clock is displayed in the Fragonard Room on a mantelpiece before a mirror, where it can be seen from all sides—just as its patron and creators intended.

Zephyrus and Flora is signed and dated 1799, shortly after Clodion's return to Paris following the Revolution. Urged on by three *putti*, Flora embraces the winged Zephyrus, god of the west wind. In the tender moment before their kiss, Zephyrus lifts a wreath of roses to crown his bride. Clodion contrasts the youthful couple's smooth flesh with Zephyrus's rippling drapery and Flora's intricate coiffure and many-petaled roses. To depict her plump attendants, Clodion skillfully exploits clay's capacity for representing soft, pliant forms. But the sculptor's greatest achievement is the work's lyrical composition.

The lovers appear weightless, with Flora stepping up to join Zephyrus on his cloud. The little cupid raising Flora's leg directs our eyes to Zephyrus's billowing drapery, which curves around his body, meeting their encircling arms and drawing us up to the wreath that symbolizes their love. For all the graceful intertwining of the two figures, Clodion maintains a narrow distance between their lips that gives the work an erotic air of anticipation.

After a long sojourn in Rome, Joseph Chinard found success as a portraitist under the consulate and empire. He completed several busts of members of the Napoleonic court, including the Empress Josephine, before returning to his native Lyons in 1808. Louis-Étienne Vincent-Marniola also hailed from Lyons, and this may have influenced his selection of Chinard as a portraitist the following year.

Once described to Napoleon as "a young man with a good head, considerable learning, a fiery heart, and considerable dignity," Vincent-Marniola was

80. Joseph Chinard (1756–1813), *Portrait of Louis-Étienne Vincent-Marniola*, 1809, terracotta, 25 ¼ x 25 ¼ x 14 ⅞ (64 x 64 x 38)

Purchased by The Frick Collection, 2004. 2004.2.01

named to the conseil d'état, the empire's foremost legislative body, in February 1809. He was not yet twenty-nine. Even within Napoleon's famously youthful administrative corps, this was a meteoric ascent, and the portrait appears to have been commissioned to commemorate this event.

Chinard's bust is a tour-de-force of modeling in clay. Vincent-Marniola's handsome—and surely somewhat idealized—features are punctuated by startlingly veristic details. The thick tasseled cords tying his cloak seem to hang with real weight, while the intricately pounced lace jabot falls lightly on his chest. Chinard modeled the eyes without irises, as though his subject were an ancient god or hero (albeit one in contemporary court dress). The slight turn of Vincent-Marniola's striking head and the suggestion of a far-off gaze combine to give the sitter an air of responsibility confidently borne.

This bust was probably the finished model for a final version in marble. However, Vincent-Marniola's death in October 1809 meant that the commission was never completed. The portrait remained in his family home for nearly two centuries before its acquisition by the Frick in 2004.

Decorative Arts

The majority of Henry Clay Frick's decorative arts collection was acquired during the 1914 to 1918 campaign to furnish 1 East 70th Street, after the collector and his family had moved into their new residence. Through the art dealer Joseph Duveen, in March 1915 Frick purchased fifty colorful Chinese porcelain jars and vases from the celebrated collection of the recently deceased American financier J. Pierpont Morgan. At the same time, Frick acquired about ten pieces of French eighteenth-century furniture and decorative arts from Duveen's stock, including some of the museum's gems: Gilles Joubert's *Commode* made in 1769 for one of Louis XV's daughters and a pair of deep blue Chinese porcelain jars mounted around 1745–49 with French gilt-bronze. Three months later, again through Duveen in June 1915, Frick acquired a dozen pieces of French eighteenth-century furniture and decorative objects from the Morgan collection.

June 1916 was the peak of Frick's decorative arts acquisitions. During that month, he bought a few pieces of Italian Renaissance furniture to display in the West Gallery and French eighteenth-century furniture and decorative arts for various rooms of the house, including the superb Sèvres *Potpourri Vase in the Shape of a Ship*. Duveen sold Frick the eight Boucher panels representing the Arts and Sciences (now attributed to his workshop), which the dealer-decorator agreed to install in Mrs. Frick's second-floor boudoir at cost, "supplying everything necessary to make the room complete and beautiful in every respect." Duveen also found a few pieces of French eighteenth-century furniture and many Sèvres porcelains to fulfill this promise. Frick went on to acquire forty sixteenth-century French enamels that Duveen had purchased from the Morgan collection. In order to display these works properly, Frick also bought from Duveen a group of French Renaissance furniture pieces assembled in the late nineteenth century by the celebrated French collector Maurice Chabrière-Arlès. In 1917 the enamels and furniture were installed in Frick's office at the rear of his Picture Gallery, then called the Limoges Gallery. This major collection of French Renaissance decorative arts remained in this setting until 1935, when the residence was transformed into a museum and the Renaissance furniture was placed in storage.

The decorative arts collection formed by Henry Clay Frick was enriched in the following eighty years by generous gifts from members of the Frick family and other donors. In 1965 the collection of Chinese porcelains was expanded by the gift from Childs Frick, the founder's son, of about two hundred blue-and-white porcelains. After that, only a handful of pieces were acquired until 1999 when the museum received the distinguished collection of watches and clocks from the New York collector Winthrop Kellogg Edey. This extraordinary gift of thirty-eight pieces dating from the Renaissance to the early nineteenth century and covering the art of watch and clock making in France, Germany, and the United Kingdom transformed the Frick into one of the most important public collections of European watches and clocks in

81– 82. The Boucher Room at The Frick Collection, 2010

the United States. The Winthrop Kellogg Edey Bequest was complemented in 2006 by the purchase of the 1788 *Dance of Time*, a caryatid pendulum clock by Jean-Baptiste Lepaute supported by three terracotta nymphs by the sculptor Claude Michel Clodion. Finally, in 2008 The Frick Collection enriched its holdings of Renaissance decorative arts by acquiring its first piece of Italian maiolica, a generous gift from Dianne Modestini in memory of her husband, Mario Modestini.

Renaissance Clocks, Enamels, Ceramics, and Furniture

The decorative arts flourished throughout Europe in the sixteenth century, with the emergence of new techniques, royal and aristocratic commissions on an unprecedented scale, and an international exchange of motifs and styles facilitated by the circulation of prints. This rich component of Renaissance material culture between 1530 and 1600 is superbly represented at The Frick Collection. In France, the appropriation of Italian art—through the artists and objects brought to the court of François I beginning in the 1530s and the emulation of Italian art by French craftsmen throughout the century—promoted a complete renewal of the decorative repertoire and gave rise to the defining characteristics of the French Renaissance.

In the long history of clock making, one of the most significant innovations was that of the spring-driven timekeeper—a type of clock powered by a coiled spring instead of by weight, made possible by the invention of a device called the "fusee." It was undoubtedly being used in clocks by 1470, and one of the earliest known examples is a gilt-brass *Table Clock* in The Frick Collection made in Aix-en-Provence about 1530 by the French clockmaker Pierre de Fobis. It is not known whether de Fobis made his clock cases himself, had a case maker in his workshop, or employed independent case makers; in any event, this case's hexagonal shape and ribbed dome reflect a knowledge of classical architecture, repurposed here in miniature form. Its ornamentation is also an early example of the French appropriation of Italian Renaissance motifs. The six faces of the case feature a geometrical composition with acanthus scrolls, classical urns, winged heads, and tiny figures whose limbs turn into elegant foliage. The initials "IM" found on each face may refer to the original owner, perhaps Jean Martin, who was instrumental in importing Renaissance architectural ideas from Italy to France. Martin's translations into French of Vitruvius, Serlio, and Alberti offered artisans, as well as architects, an education in classicism and a wealth of source material.

In late fifteenth-century Limoges, a long-standing center of metalwork and medieval enameling in western France, a new enameling technique emerged by which craftsmen created plaques and tableware with the subtle modeling of oil painting, the vivid colors of stained glass, and the gleaming luminosity unique to the medium of enamel. With expert handling of pointed tools and tiny spatulas and brushes, pastes of powdered glass in different colors were applied to a copper support, fired, and cooled in multiple stages so that they would vitrify and harden into a smooth, glassy surface. Although their manufacture was concentrated in the family-run studios of Limoges, painted enamels, as these works were called, enjoyed great demand throughout sixteenth-century France, serving purposes of devotion and decoration in wealthy households and family chapels.

The *Double Triptych with Scenes from the Passion of Christ* bears the name of the paterfamilias of the Pénicaud enamelers, Nardon Pénicaud. While based on some of Nardon's early designs, it was probably produced by a younger member of his workshop even after his death. The individual scenes, whose

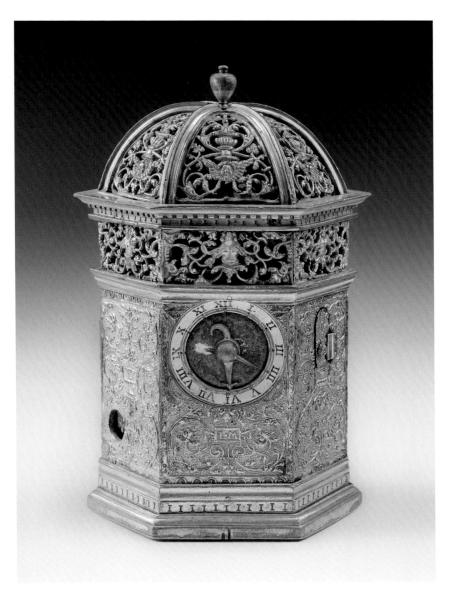

83. Pierre de Fobis (1506–1575), *Table Clock*, probably Aix-en-Provence, c. 1530, gilt-brass and blue enamel, 5 high (12.8)

Bequest from Winthrop Kellogg Edey 1999. 1999.5.129

composition derives in part from the engraved Passion series by the fifteenth-century artist Martin Schongauer, sit in a brilliant visual and thematic arrangement. Two scenes of suffering and physical burden at left—Christ Carrying the Cross and the Deposition—are contrasted with images of triumph at right: the Harrowing of Hell, in which Christ tramples the devil, and the Resurrection, in which he admonishes the soldiers at his feet, likening them to the demons in the plaque above. An exceptional brilliance, achieved with the extensive use of silver foil beneath the translucent colored enamel, suits this altarpiece's function of facilitating prayer and encouraging empathy. For the sarcophagus in the Entombment scene, the enameler applied an irregular layer of white over areas of shimmering purple and green to mimic the crystalline quality of marble. In the insets of the tomb, tiny rectangles of silver foil between layers of enamel create the effect of stone porphyry, a response perhaps to the use of such materials in other decorative art objects of the period.

Léonard Limousin, an enameler of Limoges active in the 1520s–70s, transcended the traditional boundaries of his profession, achieving individual fame on an international level. Introduced at the court of François I at Fontainebleau in the 1530s, he was named "enameler to the king" by Henri II in 1548, and his

84. Nardon Pénicaud (c. 1470?–1571),
*Double Triptych with Scenes from the
Passion of Christ*, Limoges, mid-16th
century, enamel on copper, upper
central plaque 5 ½ x 10 ⅞ (14 x 27.7);
upper wings 5 ½ x 5 (14 x 12.7); lower
central plaque 9 ¾ x 11 ⅓ (24.9 x 28.7);
lower wings 9 ¾ x 5 (24.9 x 12.7)

1916.4.03

85. Léonard Limousin (c. 1505–
1575/77), *Presumed Portrait of Antoine
de Bourbon, King of Navarre,*
Limoges, c. 1560, enamel on copper,
5 ⅛ x 4 ¼ (13 x 10.8)

1916.4.18

presence at Fontainebleau exposed him to an array of contemporary art. The *Presumed Portrait of Antoine de Bourbon, King of Navarre*, the father of the future 85 Henri IV, king of France—made shortly after midcentury and small enough to be held in one hand—demonstrates Limousin's ability to render faces in works that emulate the drawn and painted portraits of the court artists Jean Clouet (1480–1541) and his son François (1510–1572). Over a dark ground he applied thin layers of white enamel in varying degrees of thickness to create the illusion of shadow at the temple and the recess of the eye and the slight creasing of the skin in the forehead. He animated the eyes by varying the pale blue color of the irises, rendered the tiny hairs of the beard with the finest of brushes, and, before the last stage of firing, applied touches of iron red wash to create the blush of the cheeks. Finally, with hatching in gold along the top and right side of the plaque, he created a trompe-l'oeil framing device, a common feature of the tapestries he would have seen at Fontainebleau.

The same techniques characterize the Frick's *Triumph of the Eucharist and* 86 *of the Catholic Faith*, Limousin's group portrait of the Guise family, commissioned by Charles de Guise (1524–1574), cardinal of Lorraine, who appears at center in a red robe and biretta. The plaque features his personal emblem

86. Léonard Limousin (c. 1505–1575/77), *Triumph of the Eucharist and of the Catholic Faith*, Limoges, c. 1560s–70s, enamel on copper, 7 5/8 x 9 7/8 (19.2 x 25.1)

1916.4.18

and motto: an ivy-covered obelisk bearing the Latin phrase TE STANTE VIREBO ("With you standing, I shall flourish"). He walks side by side with his late father, Claude, first duc de Guise, who gazes adoringly, even deferentially, at his son. Behind them, a chariot carrying Charles's mother, Antoinette de Bourbon, tramples a group of Protestant heretics while she displays the chalice and host, rendered in gold foil laid between layers of enamel. Representing the triumph of the Catholic church's doctrine of transubstantiation, a central issue of the Counter-Reformation and the French Wars of Religion, the plaque is a private retelling of Charles's shifting religious ideals and political struggles. The Calvinists' resistance to his proposed compromise—a Gallic form of Catholicism that would have embraced some Protestant elements while upholding the traditional belief in the Eucharist and, he hoped, maintain the unity and peace of France—was communicated in no uncertain terms at Poissy in 1561. The ensuing alienation of the Guises from court and increasing violence between Protestants and Catholics motivated the cardinal to embrace his opponents' portrayal of him as one who crushed Protestants rather than reach a compromise with them. At the center of the plaque, Charles holds a book, presumably a Bible, while his father places his hand on his sword: spiritualism and military might are unified in their service to the church. For this composition commissioned by an exceptionally learned patron of the arts, Limousin took, as his model, the famous engraving *Quos Ego* by the Italian printmaker Marcantonio Raimondi (c. 1480–c. 1534).

Like Limoges, other provincial cities of sixteenth-century France became specialized centers of production of distinctive types of decorative objects, such as a rare type of earthenware associated with the small southwestern town of Saint-Porchaire, a region rich in the kaolin white clay used to make such elaborately decorated wares. Only about seventy authentic Saint-Porchaire pieces are known today, and their technical and ornamental similarities suggest a rather small production, concentrated in the hands of a few craftsmen, perhaps a single family, over a period of less than fifty years, between 1525 and 1570. Such ceramics were surely linked to the royal court, despite the distance of the center of their production from Paris and Fontainebleau. They were courtly objects, difficult and expensive to produce and far too fragile for daily use.

A Saint-Porchaire *Ewer with Interlace Decoration and Applied Reliefs* in The Frick Collection is a perfect example of the art form, which flourished around 1550. Its tall, rounded shape emulates the works of contemporary French and Italian silver- and goldsmiths. The inlaid geometric ornament, which recalls Arabic arts such as the decoration of Middle Eastern damascened metalware, may derive from a printed source as well. The *Ewer* is embellished with applied motifs including chimeras, masks, salamanders, and a frog—elements that were part of the rich and playful vocabulary of French Renaissance design.

In Italy, as in France, the sixteenth century was characterized by the demand for luxurious furnishings and tableware of supreme refinement for display in palaces and wealthy households. Among the decorative arts produced in Renaissance Italy was a tin-glazed earthenware of medieval origin known today as maiolica. A dish in The Frick Collection, made around 1565–75 in the workshop of the Fontana family in the central Italian city of Urbino—one of many centers of maiolica production in the country—features at its center a narrative scene depicting the Judgment of Paris. According to this myth, at the marriage of Peleus and Thetis, the uninvited Goddess of Discord arrived with a golden apple inscribed "for the fairest." Aphrodite, Hera, and Athena all claimed the apple and asked Zeus to judge which of them was fairest, but Zeus, reluctant to declare a winner, commanded Paris, son of Priam, king of

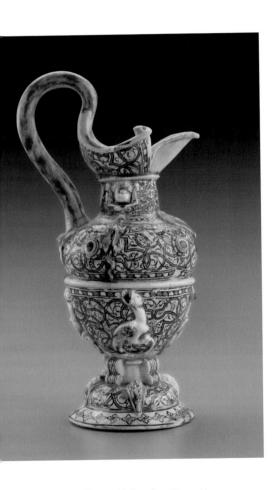

87. *Ewer with Interlace Decoration and Applied Reliefs*, France, mid-16th century, earthenware, 9 x 4 ½ (23 x 11.5)
1918.9.01

88. Workshop of Orazio Fontana,
Dish, The Judgment of Paris, Urbino,
c. 1565–75, tin-glazed earthenware
colored with metallic oxides,
16 ¾ x 2 ⅛ (42.6 x 5.4)

Gift of Dianne Dwyer Modestini in memory of her
husband, Mario Modestini. 2008.17.01

Troy, to judge the case. This scene represents the moment when Paris presents the golden apple to Aphrodite.

As maiolica painters often did, the maker of this dish based its elaborate composition on an existing model, an engraving by Marcantonio Raimondi made around 1517–20 after a drawing by Raphael. The scene is surrounded by delicate grotesques: bizarre and playful creatures, painted in bright colors on a white ground. This type of decoration appeared in the maiolica workshops of Urbino in the early 1560s and immediately became the specialty of Orazio Fontana. It derives from a set of prints known as *Les Petites Grotesques* published in 1550 and 1562 by the French architect Jacques Androuet Du Cerceau.

Seventeenth- and Eighteenth-Century Furniture and Decorative Arts

During the seventeenth and eighteenth centuries, patronage of the decorative arts expanded to satisfy the consumption of the increasingly powerful merchant and burgher classes of Western Europe, in addition to continued aristocratic demand. At various times during this period, the ongoing religious persecution of the Counter-Reformation prompted the migration of artists and artisans, and with them of their craft traditions, from one European center to another. Meanwhile, thriving trade with the East continued to bring new sources of inspiration and competition to the craftsmen of the West. Perhaps most significant was the reorientation of Europe toward France, rather than Italy, as a leading cultural center. In the 1660s the Sun King, Louis XIV, together with his minister Jean-Baptiste Colbert, established royal control over craft industries in France. Their new centralized administration and patronage quickly rendered France the leading producer of luxury goods, attracting artists and craftsmen from all over Europe and quickly developing a cultural hegemony that lasted until the downfall of the ancien régime at the end of the eighteenth century.

The Frick's gilt-brass and silver *Table Clock with Astronomical and Calendrical Dials* by David Weber, made in 1653 for his admission to the Augsburg clockmakers' guild, exemplifies this German clockmaker's knowledge of process, skill, and expertise. Although Weber chose the popular tower form for the clock's case, he demonstrated his talent and personality in its finely worked surfaces. His cast silver and brass floral arrangements and figures exhibit a brilliant combination of chasing—a technique in which the surface of the cast metal is worked to create fine detail—and repoussé—hammering the metal from the reverse side in order to create a design in relief. At this moment, clocks were generally regarded as luxury objects, satisfying their owners by keeping only approximate time and by serving as displays of wealth and taste.

A *Marquetry-Veneered Barometer Clock* made about 1690–1700 illustrates the high level of craftsmanship and originality of design of the talented artisans who served Louis XIV. The movement, by either Isaac Thuret or his son, Jacques Thuret—each having held the position of clockmaker to the king—is set within a case by André-Charles Boulle, the celebrated cabinetmaker to Louis XIV. Both the Thurets and Boulle enjoyed the privilege of occupying workshops in the Louvre Palace, which had been created by Henri IV for the use of the most favored artists employed by the crown. For the Frick's *Barometer Clock*, Boulle's workshop built the case and covered it with tortoise-shell marquetry with engraved brass and pewter arabesques and foliage patterns. It was also responsible for the design, chasing, and gilding of the highly original gilt-bronze mounts that adorn the piece. Antiquity was Boulle's main inspiration: he crowned the clock with a Greco-Roman oil lamp with a satyr's

90

89

90. David Weber (active 1623/24–1704), *Table Clock with Astronomical and Calendrical Dials*, Augsburg, probably 1653, gilt-brass and silver, 23 ⅜ high (59.4)

Bequest of Winthrop Kellogg Edey, 1999. 1999.5.144

89. Isaac (1630–1706) or Jacques (1669–1738) Thuret, case by André-Charles Boulle (1642–1732), *Marquetry-Veneered Barometer Clock*, France, c. 1690–1700, case veneered with marquetry of ebony, tortoiseshell, and brass, mounted with gilt bronzes, 45 ¼ high (114.9)

Bequest of Winthrop Kellogg Edey, 1999. 1999.5.148

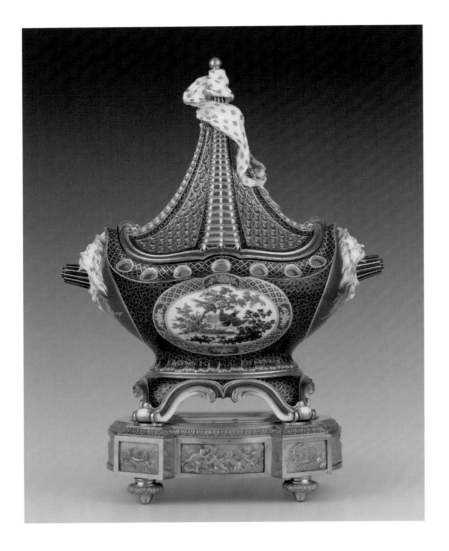

91. Royal Manufactory of Sèvres, *Potpourri Vase in the Shape of a Masted Ship*, c. 1759, soft-paste porcelain, 17 ½ x 14 ⅞ x 7 ½ (44.5 x 37.8 x 19)

1916.9.07

92. *Pair of Deep Blue Chinese Porcelain Jars with French Gilt-Bronze Mounts*, China, first half of the 18th century; gilt-bronze mounts, France, 1745–49, hard-paste porcelain colored with cobalt blue, gilt-bronze, 1915.8.41: 17 ⅞ x 18 ⅝ x 10 ¹¹⁄₁₆ (45.4 x 47.3 x 27.1); 1915.8.42: 18 ⁷⁄₁₆ x 18 ⅝ x 10 ⅝ (47 x 47.3 x 27)

1915.8.41, 1915.8.42

head and placed an Egyptian sphinx on each side of the base, which rests on spiral turrets. The beautiful bas-relief below the clock's dial represents Cronos, the Titan god of time and the ages and the father of Zeus. Boulle's embrace of the antique—Egyptian and classical—represents a central aspect of the style that prevailed during the reign of the Sun King.

A *Pair of Deep Blue Chinese Porcelain Jars with French Gilt-Bronze Mounts* from about 1745–49 epitomize the Rococo, a highly decorative style that emerged in Paris in the 1730s and remained in fashion until the 1760s. Inspired by natural forms, Rococo imagery often features bulrushes, seashells, branches of coral, marine rocks, and pearls, combined with abstract scroll motifs. Here, in the beautifully chased and gilt-bronze mounts of the Frick pieces, these motifs appear in unrealistic scale and asymmetric design.

By the late 1740s trade with China had brought to Europe large quantities of porcelain wares. These two porcelain jars reached France soon after they were made in China in the first half of the eighteenth century. Such large monochrome porcelains were especially rare and costly, yet they did not fulfill the French market's perpetual search for novelty. Innovative *marchands merciers*, the eighteenth-century merchants of luxury goods, often enriched these already luxurious objects with elaborate gilt-bronze mounts. The *marchand mercier* responsible for the creation of the Frick's vases would have engaged a bronze caster to create the mounts, fifteen elements for each jar, each cast, chased, and gilded separately. The mounts form a base and provide handles while giving the Chinese porcelains the fashionable ornaments sought by eighteenth-century French collectors.

The vogue for Asian porcelains inspired Europeans to try to produce their own, but true, hard-paste, porcelains were not produced in Europe until 1709, when the Meissen factory near Dresden succeeded in mixing kaolin (the essential white clay) with quartz feldspar; in France this did not take place until 1768. Before then, French potters produced beautiful soft-paste porcelains by mixing powdered glass, marl (refined clay), lead oxide, and chalk to produce a gleaming white material.

Under Louis XV's patronage, the celebrated royal manufactory of Sèvres became the most important soft-paste porcelain factory in Europe. Madame de Pompadour, the king's mistress, who took a special interest in the factory, succeeded in assembling a remarkable team of artists and craftsmen. Among them was the silversmith Jean-Claude Duplessis (1695–1774), who provided the factory with innovative designs, including those for a *Potpourri Vase in the Shape of a Masted Ship*, a rare version of which is in The Frick Collection. Based on a 1757 model, this masterpiece can be dated to about 1759, the year that Madame de Pompadour purchased her first potpourri ship. The early history of the Frick piece is unknown, but it certainly belonged to a wealthy aristocrat or financier, in whose home the vase would have held a mixture of dried fragrant flowers and spices to scent the air. The painters and gilders responsible for its decoration juxtaposed grounds of apple green and dark blue, the latter enriched with gold in a *caillouté* (pebble-like) pattern, and painted colorful exotic birds on the front and back reserves. Gold, an exclusive privilege of the royal manufactory, is generously applied along the contours of the piece to emphasize its bold, recognizable shape.

Fashions evolved quickly in eighteenth-century France. By 1760 the Rococo was supplanted by a more restrained style inspired by classical architecture. Although this new style had its roots in antiquity and in the classicism of Louis XIV, it developed into the elegant taste now associated with the reign of Louis XVI and Marie-Antoinette. A clock in The Frick Collection, made in 1767, seven years before Louis XVI's accession to the throne, is today

92

91

2, 93

93. Movement by Ferdinand Berthoud (1727–1807); case by Balthazar Lieutaud (active 1749[?]–1780); bronzes by Philippe Caffiéri (1714–1774), *Longcase Regulator Clock with Mounts Emblematic of Apollo*, detail (see ill. 2), 1767, oak veneered with various woods including tulipwood, kingwood, and amaranth with gilt-bronze on marble plinth, 100 x 23 ¾ (254 x 60.3)
1915.5.46

94. Made by Roger Vandercruse Lacroix (1728–1799) under the direction of Gilles Joubert (1689–1775), *Commode with Pictorial Marquetry*, France, 1769, oak veneered with various woods including maple, pearwood, bloodwood, and amaranth, gilt-bronze, marble, 35 ¾ x 73 ½ x 26 ½ (90.8 x 186.7 x 66.1)

1915.5.37, 1915.5.37

114

considered one of the most sumptuous French neoclassical longcase clocks in existence. This outstanding example is the work of three craftsmen: Ferdinand Berthoud, who was responsible for the clock's highly accurate "regulator," or movement; Balthazar Lieutaud, who designed and built the elegant case; and Philippe Caffiéri, who made the gilt-bronze mounts. To Berthoud's technical accomplishment, the cabinetmaker and sculptor added their finest efforts, together producing a supremely sophisticated object. Lieutaud veneered his neoclassically designed case with precious exotic woods such as tulipwood, kingwood, and amaranth. Caffiéri also designed his gilt bronzes in the purest neoclassical style, with ornamental elements drawn from classical architecture and subjects from Greek mythology. The sculptural group at the apex of the clock represents Apollo driving his chariot on his daily journey across the heavens.

The French court was slower to embrace the new modern style. A royal *Commode with Pictorial Marquetry* made two years after Berthoud, Lieutaud, 94 and Caffiéri's clock shows fewer signs of neoclassicism. Made in 1769 for the bedroom of Madame Victoire, daughter of Louis XV, in the château de Compiègne, it bears elements of both styles: the marquetry designs and most of the gilt bronzes are based on classical motifs, but the undulating form of the commode and the large apron mount in the center of the piece belong to the earlier Rococo style. Although archival documents attest that Gilles Joubert, who became cabinetmaker to the king in 1763 at age seventy-four, delivered this *Commode* to the court, it was actually made by other skilled craftsmen. The furnishing of royal residences demanded more objects than the elderly craftsman could provide, and Joubert often subcontracted works to cabinet-makers, including Roger Vandercruse Lacroix, whose stamp, R.V.L.C, is found in four different places on this commode. Lacroix's workshop was responsible for making the woodwork, while an unknown bronze-maker designed, cast, and chased the gilt-bronze mounts. Gilles Joubert, as cabinetmaker to the king, oversaw the many craftsmen involved in this royal commission.

Outside the royal administration, such activity fell into the hands of *marchands merciers*, like Simon-Philippe Poirier and Dominique Daguerre. In the early 1760s, Poirier received exclusive rights from the royal manufactory of Sèvres to commission porcelain plaques that could be used on furniture. In 1777 this monopoly passed to Daguerre, who is probably responsible for the design of the Frick's *Mechanical Table with Sèvres Porcelain Plaques*. Daguerre 95 relied on the cabinetmaker Martin Carlin to make this delicate table, destined for a fashionable lady. It illustrates the French fascination with mechanical devices during the second half of the eighteenth century. Brass supports hidden inside the upper portion of each of the legs allow the tabletop to be raised an additional fifteen inches. The top also pivots and tilts to become a book rest. Small supports extend from each side of the top to hold candle stands. Such adjustability and the table's small size make a useful portable writing table or a stand for the eighteenth-century practice of reading while standing.

Jean-Henri Riesener assumed the position of cabinetmaker to the king in 1774 when Gilles Joubert retired. A highly imaginative designer, he produced furniture in a refined style, while alternating surface treatments with a range of luxurious materials, including colorful marquetry patterns, Japanese lacquer, and mother of pearl. His royal appointment enabled him to commission custom gilt mounts for his furniture, resulting in fully integrated designs. Although Riesener lost this title in 1784 because of administrative changes in the *Garde-Meuble Royal*, the French administration responsible for the furnishing of royal residences, he continued to work for Marie-Antoinette. Around this time, she commissioned a *Commode* and a *Secrétaire* for one of the many 96, 97

95. Martin Carlin (c. 1730–1785), *Mechanical Table with Sèvres Porcelain Plaques*, France, c. 1781, oak veneered with maple, plaques of soft-paste porcelain, gilt-bronze, 45 ¾ x 14 ⅛ x 10 ¾ (116.2 x 35.9 x 27.3) 1915.5.62

96. Jean-Henri Riesener (1734–1806),
*Commode with Pictorial and Trellis
Marquetry*, c. 1785 and 1791, oak
veneered with various woods
including ash, bloodwood, and
amaranth, gilt-bronze, marble,
37 ¾ x 56 ¾ x 24 ⅝ (95.9 x 144.2 x 62.6)
1915.5.76

97. Jean-Henri Riesener (1734–1806),
*Secrétaire with Pictorial and Trellis
Marquetry*, c. 1785 and 1790, oak
veneered with various woods
including ash, bloodwood, and
amaranth, gilt-bronze, leather,
marble, 56 ⅜ x 45 ½ x 17 ¼
(143.2 x 115.6 x 43.8)
1915.5.75

residences that she was refurnishing in the early 1780s, possibly the château de Saint-Cloud, west of Paris. Several years later, Riesener reworked these two pieces for the queen's new apartment at the Tuileries, where the royal family was forced to reside after the Revolution began in 1789. This alteration required reducing their scale to suit the humbled queen's new abode. Riesener's solution was to shorten each piece, change the feet, and apply simpler mounts. He was no doubt pleased with the elegant results, as he took the unusual step of signing and dating the marquetry panels on each piece.

98–99 Aristocrats, financiers, and diplomats often commissioned furnishings that surpassed those destined for a royal setting. A stunning *Blue Marble Side Table with Neoclassical Mounts* in The Frick Collection is such a piece. Made in the early 1780s for Louise-Jeanne de Durfort, duchesse de Mazarin (1732–1789), it is one of the few pieces of eighteenth-century furniture made entirely in hard stone, a rare grayish-blue marble from North Africa known in France as *bleu turquin*. This table was the collaborative work of two of the greatest artists active in Paris in the 1770s–80s: its designer, the architect Jean-François-Thérèse Chalgrin, better known as the architect of the Arc de Triomphe, and the great *ciseleur-doreur* Pierre Gouthière, who cast, gilt, and chased the neoclassical bronzes. Gouthière's detailed chasing lends a naturalistic appearance to the swirling leaves, swags of fruit, and particularly the hair of the central bacchante mask. Credited with pioneering the use of matte gilding on bronze and unsurpassed in the technique, Gouthière exploited the subtle contrast between such matte surfaces and areas of burnished gilding to bring additional depth to the sculptural mounts.

98. Pierre Gouthière (1732–1813), detail of bronze on *Blue Marble Side Table*

99. Pierre Gouthière (1732–1813), bronzes; designed by Jean-François-Thérèse Chalgrin (1739–1811), *Blue Marble Side Table with Neoclassical Mounts*, 1781, bleu turquin marble and gilt bronze, 37 ½ x 81 ⅛ x 27 (95.3 x 206.1 x 68.6), shown in situ in the North Hall
1915.5.59

Asian Porcelain and Carpets

Asian art is represented at the Frick by a large collection of Chinese porcelain and a handful of Persian and Indian rugs. One of the greatest works of art to 100 have survived from the Mughal period in the Collection is a carpet designed and produced in the first half of the seventeenth century in northern India. On a rich bluish-red ground, a row of alternating varieties of green and flowering trees—including cypress, various kinds of broad-leaf trees, and yellow peachlike and pink plumlike trees—appears at center, surrounded by a large border woven with stylized flowers, leaves, buds, and palmettes. Although the design is symmetrical and repetitive, no one motif is identical to another, so that the composition appears animated. The delicate polychromatic shading and refined treatment of the foliage, which find parallels in Indian miniature paintings, were achieved by the use of particularly expensive materials, notably imported silk (for the warps and wefts), costly dyes exclusively available in India, and the rarest natural materials used for carpet weaving: the very fine hair of Himalayan goats, known as pashmina. In fact, this carpet is a small fragment of a much larger one, and its original size and extraordinary quality leave no doubt that it was made in one of the official imperial workshops for a member of the Mughal imperial family, or someone very close to it.

Two early eighteenth-century Asian artworks in the Collection were made in China, most certainly in the imperial kilns at Jingdezhen, in Jiangxi province. The late seventeenth and early eighteenth centuries were a particularly innovative period of production, which saw the development of new techniques and ornamentation. One of the most important contributions was the invention of the overglaze enamel palettes known as *famille verte* because 101 they are dominated by translucent green enamels. The *Two Figures of Ladies on Stands* are decorated with a colorful mix of green, red, yellow, aubergine, and blue enamels in a pattern of naturalistic motifs such as chrysanthemum,

100. Carpet with Tree Pattern, northern India, c. 1650, silk and pashmina, 89 ⅓ x 75 ⅝ (226.8 x 192)

1916.10.07

rose blossoms, and flying storks combined with abstract elements like the large *wan* (swastika) shape—a Buddhist symbol promising good fortune—that is repeated on the porcelain bases.

These porcelain ladies represent ideal female beauty, with the most perfect physical traits as defined by the writer and aesthetician Li Yu (1611–1680): egg-shaped rather than round faces, eyebrows lightly curved like the leaves of a willow tree, lips resembling cherries, and slim, supple, curved bodies also resembling willow trees. Their delicate hands seem to be offering a fruit or a flower, in China the sign of a good wish addressed from a woman to a man. Although a product of late seventeenth- and early eighteenth-century Chinese culture, these two figural ceramics were probably made for export to the West and not for Chinese consumption. Their large size, however, made them a particularly fragile item to ship, and only a few ever reached Europe intact.

101. Two Figures of Ladies on Stands, China, probably Jingdezhen, in Jiangxi province, early 18th century, hard-paste porcelain decorated with colored enamels, 38 high (96.5)

1918.8.39

Works on Paper

Local artists' reproductive prints of paintings and drawings were among Henry Clay Frick's first purchases as a young man starting out in Pittsburgh in the 1870s and 1880s. These affordable images nurtured his innate love of pictures and enhanced his modest surroundings. As a successful entrepreneur in the 1890s, Frick began to buy paintings and works on paper by contemporary Salon and Barbizon artists. Between 1897 and 1906 he added ten pastels by Jean-François Millet—some of the finest drawings he acquired. These, however, remained at his Pittsburgh home when he moved to New York City and are now in the Frick Art & Historical Center in Pittsburgh.

By the time Frick settled permanently in New York in the early 1900s as a leading industrialist and a major collector, his pursuit of masterpieces of European painting took precedence over his earlier interest in works on paper. It was only when the construction of his Fifth Avenue house was under way in 1913 that he turned again to prints and drawings, though in a minor way, and largely for the purpose they had first served—as part of the décor of his living quarters. Between 1913 and 1916, Frick purchased ten drawings. Two portrait studies and an oil and chalk landscape by Gainsborough and three pen *104* and ink sketches by Rembrandt came from the famous John Postle Heseltine collection in London and were purchased through Knoedler & Co. In 1916 Frick bought three of Whistler's Venice pastels from Richard Canfield, a New York casino owner who had sold him three paintings by the same artist the previous year. He also bought a portrait of a woman in gouache and chalk by Daniel Gardner, a lesser-known eighteenth-century English artist.

With such a small base of drawings, the trustees and directors of The Frick Collection had little to guide them in developing this area, or even incentive to do so. Nothing was added until the renowned collection of Henry Oppenheimer came up for sale at Christie's in London in July 1936. Seven Old Master drawings were acquired from that sale, the largest single addition made to this area of the collection. The Frick's first director, Frederick Mortimer Clapp, selected works by Altdorfer, Niklaus Manuel Deutsch, Goya, Pisanello, *102–103* Rubens, Bernard Striegel, and Titian. For years drawings again receded into the background as paintings continued to be added on a regular basis. In 1959 the trustees bought Ingres's study for the *Comtesse d'Haussonville*, one of the most beloved paintings in the museum. From then on the informal acquisition policy of the Board has been to add only drawings—by purchase or through gift—that relate in some way to existing paintings and sculpture in the collection. Another thirteen have been acquired from 1960 to the present. Included in this group are five works that were again purchased because of the remarkable, uncommon nature of the sale: three drawings by Claude Lorrain from *105* an album that had come to light in 1957 and two beautiful pastel portraits by Jean-Baptiste Greuze.

In 2010 the Frick's collection of nearly thirty drawings was expanded again by one-third its size. Former director Charles Ryskamp, an avid collector of

102–103. Francisco de Goya y Lucientes (1746–1828), *The Anglers,* 1812–20, brush and brown wash, lifted in places, possibly with some slight traces of scraping on paper, 7 ¾ x 5 ⁵⁄₁₆ (19.7 x 13.5)
1936.3.60

works on paper and a champion of drawing connoisseurship, left by bequest to The Frick Collection ten sheets to be selected by the director and curators. While he served as director of the Frick, Charles Ryskamp established the Cabinet for works on paper (as well as small paintings and objects) and strongly promoted drawing exhibitions in the Lower-Level Exhibition Galleries.

Three of the ten works chosen—a landscape in pencil by Pierre-Étienne Rousseau, an early academic nude by Hilaire-Germain-Edgar Degas, and a pen-and-ink character study by Giovanni Battista Tiepolo—bring new aspects of artists already represented in the collection by oil paintings. Seven others, from Pierre-Joseph Redouté's watercolor on vellum of plums of 1802 to the Victorian master Sir Edwin Landseer's undated gouache and watercolor of otter hounds, were selected for their quality and art-historical significance and as testimonies to Charles Ryskamp's particular interest in French and British art of the seventeenth and eighteenth centuries. Among other artists represented in the bequest are Eugène Delacroix, George Stubbs, Henry Fuseli, William Blake, and Sir David Wilkie. Most of the drawings were exhibited in *Varieties of Experience: Drawings from the Collection of Charles Ryskamp* at the Yale Center for British Art in 2010.

105. Claude Lorrain (1600–1682), *Heroic Landscape* (recto), 1655–58, pen, iron-gall ink, brown wash, gray wash and white heightening on laid paper, 11 ⅞ x 15 ¹¹⁄₁₆ (30.1 x 39.9)
Purchased by The Frick Collection, 1982. 1982.3.124

104. Thomas Gainsborough (1727–1788), *Study of a Woman Facing Right, Possibly Ann Ford (Later Mrs. Philip Thicknesse)*, c. 1760, black chalk (with evidence of chalk dipped in oil) and pencil on buff laid paper, 14 ⅛ x 10 ⅜ (35.9 x 26.4)
1913.3.07

Index

Bibliography

General Reading

Bailey, Colin B. *Building the Frick Collection: An Introduction to the House and Its Collections.* New York: The Frick Collection in association with Scala, 2006.

Ballon, Hilary. *Mr. Frick's Palace.* New York: The Frick Collection, 2009.

The Frick Collection: An Illustrated Catalogue. 9 vols. New York: Princeton University Press.

Vol. I, *American, British, Dutch, Flemish and German Paintings*, Bernice Davidson, 1968.

Vol. II, *French, Italian and Spanish Paintings*, Bernice Davidson assisted by Edgar Munhall, 1968.

Vol. III, *Italian Sculpture*, John Pope-Hennessy with Anthony F. Radcliffe, 1970.

Vol. IV, *German, Netherlandish, French and British Sculpture*, John Pope-Hennessy, assisted by Anthony F. Radcliffe, and Terence W. I. Hodgkinson, 1970.

Vol. V, *Italian and French Furniture*, David DuBon and Theodore Dell, 1992.

Vol. VI, *French Furniture and Gilt Bronzes*, Theodore Dell, 1992.

Vol. VII, *Oriental and French Porcelains*, John A. Pope and Marcelle Brunet, 1974.

Vol. VIII, *Enamels, Rugs, and Silver*, Philippe Verdier, Maurice S. Dimand, and Kathryn C. Buhler, 1977.

Vol. IX, *Drawings, Prints, and Later Acquisitions*, Bernice F. Davidson, Susan Grace Galassi, Edgar Munhall, and David P. Becker, et al., 2003.

Handbook of Paintings: The Frick Collection. New York: The Frick Collection in association with Scala, 2004.

Ryskamp, Charles, Bernice Davidson, Susan Grace Galassi, Edgar Munhall, and Nadia Tscherny. *Art in The Frick Collection: Paintings, Sculpture, Decorative Arts.* New York: Harry N. Abrams in association with The Frick Collection, 1996.

Sanger, Martha Frick Symington. *Henry Clay Frick: An Intimate Portrait.* New York: Abbeville Press Publishers, 1998.

Sanger, Martha Frick Symington. *Helen Clay Frick: Bittersweet Heiress.* Pittsburgh: University of Pittsburgh Press, 2006.

Publications Relevant to the Collection

Allen, Denise, with Peta Motture. *Andrea Riccio: Renaissance Master of Bronze.* Exh. cat. New York: The Frick Collection in association with Philip Wilson, London, 2008.

Andrewes, William J. H. *The Art of the Timekeeper: Masterpieces from the Winthrop Edey Bequest.* Exh. cat. New York: The Frick Collection, 2001.

Borchert, Till-Holger. *Memling's Portraits.* Exh. cat. Amsterdam: Ludion, 2005.

Brown, Jonathan, and Susan Grace Galassi. *El Greco: Themes & Variations.* New York: The Frick Collection, 2001.

Brown, Jonathan, and Susan Grace Galassi. *Goya's Last Works.* Exh. cat. New York: The Frick Collection, in association with Yale University Press, 2006.

Cohen, Steven, and Nobuko Kajitani. *Gardens of Eternal Spring: Two Newly Conserved Seventeenth-Century Mughal Carpets in The Frick Collection.* Exh. cat. New York: The Frick Collection, 2006.

Davidson, Bernice. *Severo and the Sea-Monsters.* New York: The Frick Collection, 1997.

Elam, Caroline. *Roger Fry & the Re-Evaluation of Piero della Francesca.* New York: The Frick Collection, 2004.

Flora, Holly. *Cimabue and Early Italian Devotional Painting.* Exh. cat. New York: The Frick Collection, 2006.

Galassi, Susan Grace. *Chinese Blue-and-White Porcelain in The Frick Collection.* New York: The Frick Collection, 1992.

Galassi, Susan Grace, with Ann Hoenigswald, Malcolm Park, Juliet Wilson-Bareau. *Manet's The Dead Toreador and The Bullfight: Fragments of a Lost Salon Painting Reunited.* New York: The Frick Collection, 1999.

Hope, Charles. *Giorgione or Titian?: History of a Controversy.* New York: The Frick Collection, 2003.

MacDonald, Margaret F., Susan Grace Galassi and Aileen Ribeiro. *Whistler, Women, & Fashion.* New York: The Frick Collection in association with Yale University Press, 2003.

Munhall, Edgar. *Little Notes Concerning Watteau's Portal of Valenciennes.* New York: The Frick Collection, 1992.

Munhall, Edgar. *Whistler and Montesquiou: The Butterfly and the Bat.* New York and Paris: The Frick Collection and Flammarion, 1995.

Munhall, Edgar. *Ingres and the Comtesse d'Haussonville.* New York: The Frick Collection, 1998.

Munhall, Edgar. *Greuze the Draftsman.* Exh. cat. London: Merrell, in association with The Frick Collection, 2002.

Poulet, Anne L. *Clodion Terracottas in North American Collections.* Exh. cat. New York: The Frick Collection, 1984.

Reff, Theodore. *Manet's Incident in a Bullfight.* New York: The Frick Collection, 2005.

Salomon, Xavier F. *Veronese's Allegories: Virtue, Love, and Exploration in Renaissance Venice.* New York: The Frick Collection, 2006.

Smentek, Kristel. *Rococo Exotic: French Mounted Porcelains and the Allure of the East.* New York: The Frick Collection, 2007.

Vignon, Charlotte. *Exuberant Grotesques: Renaissance Maiolica from the Fontana Workshop.* New York: The Frick Collection, 2009.

Published with the support of Fondation BNP PARIBAS

Books in print

AGEN	The Musée des Beaux-Arts
AIX-EN-PROVENCE	The Musée Granet
ALBI	The Musée Toulouse-Lautrec
AMIENS	The Museum of Picardy
ANTIBES	The Picasso Museum
ARRAS	The Musée des Beaux-Arts
BAYONNE	The Bonnat Museum
BESANÇON	The Museum of Fine Arts and Archaeology
BORDEAUX	The Museum of Aquitaine
BOURG-EN-BRESSE	The Monastère Royal de Brou
CAEN	The Mémorial de Caen
CAEN	The Museum of Fine Arts
CAMBRAI	The Musée de Cambrai
CASTRES	The Musée Goya
CHALON-SUR-SAÔNE	The Musée Nicéphore Niépce
CHANTILLY	The Musée Condé
COLMAR	The Unterlinden Museum
COMPIÈGNE	The Imperial Palace
DIJON	The Museum of Fine Arts
DOUAI	The Musée de la Chartreuse
ECOUEN	The Château
FONTAINEBLEAU	The Château
GRENOBLE	The Museum of Art
LILLE	The Palais des Beaux-Arts
LIMOGES	The National Museum Adrien Dubouché
LYONS	The Museum of Fine Arts
LYONS	The Textile Museum
MARSEILLES	The Musée d'Arts africains, océaniens, amérindiens
MONTPELLIER	The Musée Fabre
MULHOUSE	The National Automobile Museum (Schlumpf Collection)
NANCY	The Museum of Fine Arts
NANTES	The Museum of Fine Arts
ORLÉANS	The Museum of Fine Arts
PARIS	Bibliothèque Nationale
PARIS	The Musée des Arts et Métiers
PARIS	The Carnavalet Museum
PARIS	The Gustave Moreau Museum
PARIS	The Musée national du Moyen Age
PARIS	The National Museum of Modern Art Cabinet d'Art graphique
PARIS	The National Museum of Modern Art Paintings & Sculptures
PARIS	The Nissim de Camondo Museum
POITIERS	The Museums of Poitiers
QUIMPER	The Museum of Fine Arts
REIMS	The Musée des Beaux-Arts
LA RÉUNION	The Musée Saint-Denis
ROUEN	The Museum of Fine Arts
LES SABLES D'OLONNE	The Musée de l'Abbaye Sainte-Croix
SAINT-ETIENNE	The Museum of Modern Art
SAINT-GERMAIN-EN-LAYE	The Musée des Antiquités nationales
SAINT-TROPEZ	The Annonciade Museum
VERSAILLES	The Palace
DÜSSELDORF	The museum kunst palast
LISBON	The National Coach Museum
LISBON	The Orient Museum
LOS ANGELES	Los Angeles County Museum of Art
MONTREAL	The Museum of Fine Arts

Series Design Concept
Stéphan Alberty

Design Production
Tony Waddingham

Editing
Elaine Koss and Julie Di Filippo

Photography
Don Swanson ill. 2; Frick Art & Historical
Center, Pittsburgh ill. 7, 15; The Frick
Collection / Frick Art Reference Library
Archives ill. 8, 11, 12, 17, 18.
All other images are by Michael Bodycomb.

Production
Ludion, Antwerp

Dimensions are in inches, followed in
parentheses by centimeters; height precedes
width precedes depth.

ISBN 978-0-912114-52-1 (US edition)
ISBN 978-2-7118-57197 (European edition)
Depot legal : April 2011
Reprinted : February 2012, March 2013

Printed in Spain